ESCAPE FROM AUSCHWITZ

ESCAPE FROM AUSCHWITZ

ANDREI POGOZHEV

Translators
Vladimir Krupnik, John Armstrong

English text
Christopher Summerville

Publication made possible by
www.iremember.ru

Pen & Sword
MILITARY

First published in Great Britain in 2007 by
Pen & Sword Military
an imprint of
Pen & Sword Books Ltd
47 Church Street
Barnsley
South Yorkshire
S70 2AS

ISBN 978 1 84415 594 1

A CIP catalogue record for this book is
available from the British Library.

Typeset in Sabon by
Phoenix Typesetting, Auldgirth, Dumfriesshire

Printed and bound in England by
Biddles Ltd, King's Lynn

Pen & Sword Books Ltd incorporates the imprints of Pen & Sword
Aviation, Pen & Sword Maritime, Pen & Sword Military, Wharncliffe
Local History, Pen & Sword Select, Pen & Sword Military Classics and
Leo Cooper.

For a complete list of Pen & Sword titles please contact
PEN & SWORD BOOKS LIMITED
47 Church Street, Barnsley, South Yorkshire, S70 2AS, England
E-mail: enquiries@pen-and-sword.co.uk
Website: www.pen-and-sword.co.uk

Contents

List of Plates

Plates appear between pages 96 and 97

Maria and Andrei Pogozhev, 1940.

In the first year of the war around 3,400,000 Soviet soldiers were captured. According to Christian Streit in *Keine Kameraden: Die Wehrmacht utid die sowjetischen Kriegsgefatigetieiz, 1941–1945* at the end of January 1942 only 1,400,000 survived. The rest were murdered or died from hunger, cold or sickness.

The bodies of the prisoners who didn't survive the journey to the camp were laid out in front of the railway cars.

Barbed wire and electric fences surrounded the camp.

The camp gates with the German sign saying 'Labour Makes You Free'.

A prisoner's uniform.

Reichsführer SS Himmler inspecting the construction of the 'Buna-Werke' plant at Dvory near Auschwitz.

Birkenau prisoners work on the construction of new camp buildings in 1942 or 1943.

Members of the Sonderkommando burning corpses on pyres in pits in 1944.

Birkenau: in this stable intended for 52 horses, 700–1000 prisoners were forced to live.

The 'Wall of Death' between the 10th and 11th blocks where prisoners were executed.

Auschwitz prisoners after liberation by Soviet troops.

Piles of bones and clothes – all that remained of the 1.5 million people exterminated in Auschwitz.

Andrei Pogozhev.

Tattoos on the chest of Andrei Pogozhev which were made before his escape, to hide his camp number. The scars on his left wrist show where it was broken by a guard's bullet. The dark patch of the tattoo hides the marks showing the year of his birth.

Pavel Sten'kin.

Aerial photo of Auschwitz.

Foreword

On 27 January 1945 the Red Army liberated Auschwitz, the largest concentration camp in German-controlled territory. When Soviet troops arrived only a few thousand sick and starving survivors remained: thousands more – perhaps up to 60,000 – had been marched west by the retreating Germans. Meanwhile, it became clear that slaughter on an unprecedented scale had taken place. Among the grim remains discovered by the Russians were 7 tons of women's hair, large quantities of human teeth – from which gold fillings had been removed – and tens of thousands of children's outfits.

Despite repeated attempts by the Polish Underground to inform the world of the horrors taking place at Auschwitz, the news officially broke on 8 May 1945, when a Soviet commission, aided by Polish, French and Czech experts, revealed the full extent of Nazi crimes against humanity. Initial Allied estimates claimed 4 million men, women and children had been murdered in the camp. At Nuremberg, SS Camp Commandant Rudolf Höss suggested 3 million. Later, officials from the Auschwitz Museum revised these figures to approximately 1.5 million, about 90 per cent of whom were Jews.

Auschwitz was the German name for Oświęcim in south-western Poland, a small town on the banks of the Vistula, some 75 miles from Kraków. The camp was constructed 1½ miles out of town, on the eastern bank of the river, around a dilapidated complex of old barracks and horse stables. Work began in 1940, the camp's original purpose being to house Polish political prisoners following the German occupation. In April 1940 SS Captain Rudolf Höss – an experienced concentration camp administrator – arrived with orders from SS-Reichsführer

Heinrich Himmler to expand the site: Auschwitz had been earmarked as a forced labour camp for an enslaved Polish populace – the adjunct to a proposed 'model' Nazi town.

But the designated role of Auschwitz soon changed. Three major factors contributed to this. First, Operation *Barbarossa* – the German invasion of the Soviet Union in June 1941 – had bagged a large number of Soviet POWs for internment. Second, the Nazi war of extermination against the Jews by conventional means (i.e. shooting, hanging and so on) was proving both a drain on military resources and morale, leading to calls for a 'solution'. Third, the Adult Euthanasia Programme (AEP) in Germany was setting a precedent for wholesale liquidation of individuals deemed unfit or undesirable by the State. Thus, Auschwitz was to become a vast concentration camp holding tens of thousands of prisoners from all over the Reich, detained on the grounds of nationality, race, religion, political (and sexual) orientation. Meanwhile, in a remote spot north-west of the main complex, a second camp would be constructed using Soviet slave labour. Known as 'Birkenau' or 'Auschwitz II' its purpose was mass extermination, primarily of Jews.

But Höss soon realized that in order to meet Berlin's demands, Auschwitz-Birkenau would have to become a factory of death, capable of killing and cremating thousands of human beings each day. And so gas chambers, crematoria and subsidiary labour camps were all established, serviced by rail and maintained by 'work teams' or 'labour crews' recruited from the inmates.

As for the latter, they were controlled by a divide-and-rule policy that pitted prisoner against prisoner. To this end a camp hierarchy was established with 'Aryans' (i.e. Germans from the greater Reich) on top, Jews at the bottom, and Slavs in between. Further discrimination took the form of colour-coded badges indicating a prisoner's 'offence'. For example: green for common criminals, pink for homosexuals, purple for Jehovah's Witnesses, black for Gypsies and yellow for Jews. Finally, a number of prisoners were recruited as overseers – the dreaded 'Kapos' and block supervisors – tasked with ensuring slavish obedience to the camp regime, in return for certain privileges. Many of these men were even more brutal than their SS masters.

Escape from Auschwitz was rare, though not unheard of. That said, escapes were not always welcomed by the general camp population, which suffered savage reprisals after every attempt – successful or otherwise. In all some 700 escapes were effected but around 400 ended in recapture. Those unlucky enough to get caught were usually paraded around the camp prior to execution with a sign round their necks declaring: 'Hurray – I'm back!' The favoured method of murdering would-be escapers was by starvation or beating. Any successful escape was usually followed by the murder of the absconder's comrades. Inmates thus found themselves restrained by psychological barriers as well as physical ones.

The first transport of Soviet POWs arrived at Auschwitz within weeks of *Barbarossa*. These were commissars – political officers attached to Red Army units – and within days all had been murdered. The next transport consisted of 600 POWs and on 3 September 1941 they – and some 250 Poles – were gassed to death in the first large-scale use of 'Zyklon-B', a commercially produced delousing agent. In this sense the Soviets were used as lab rats while the camp administration experimented with dosage. Sealed up in 'Block 11', these men took two days to die.

By October 1941 some 10,000 Soviet POWs were at Auschwitz, herded into a specially prepared 'Russiche Kriegsgefagenen Arbeitslager' or 'Russian POW Labour Camp' – including Andrei Pogozhev, the author of this book. Shortly afterwards Pogozhev and his comrades were put to work on the Birkenau construction site. Conditions for the POWs were appalling, Soviets being treated even more harshly than the Poles. Forced to work in simple fatigues (and without underwear), the Soviets endured winter temperatures of minus thirty-five degrees Celsius, many succumbing to sickness or starvation. Others were simply beaten to death. The mortality rate was so high that on 4 November 1941 some 352 Russians died.

According to the memoirs of Camp Commandant Rudolf Höss

(*Wspomnienia Rudolfa Hoessa, komendanta obozu Oswiecimskiego*, Widawnictwo prawnicze Warszawa 1956), a 'mass escape' of Soviet POWs took place in 1942:

> Most of them were shot, but still many of them escaped. The ones who were captured stated that fear of being sent to the gas chambers - when it was announced that the prisoners would be transferred to the new part of the camp - caused this escape. They didn't believe the information about the transfer, assuming they were being deceived, although nobody wanted to send them to the gas chambers. Of course they knew about the extermination of Soviet 'politruks' and commissars and were afraid to share their fate.

The Soviet breakout is also mentioned in Danuta Czech's Auschwitz Journal (published in *Zeszyty Oswiencimskie vol. 3*, wydawnictwo panstwowego muzeum w Osweiecimiu 1958), which states that 'fifty POWs from [a] penal company made the escape', adding that 'As a result of the pursuit thirteen prisoners were shot and nine managed to escape.' But despite Czech's journal, it seems that only five escapees actually made it to freedom, including Andrei Pogozhev and his comrade, Pavel Sten'kin.

Both Pogozhev and Sten'kin later recorded independent testimonies regarding Auschwitz and the Soviet escape. These accounts vary in detail – nothing unusual in memoirs written long after the events they describe – with Pogozhev placing much emphasis on patriotism as a motivating factor among Soviet POWs. This can perhaps be explained by the fact that, having been separated from Sten'kin during the escape, Pogozhev eventually fell into the hands of the Soviet secret police, the NKVD. Following Stalin's Order 270 (dated 16 August 1941), which stated that 'There are no Russian prisoners of war, only traitors', Pogozhev felt obliged to stress his loyalty to the Soviet Union.

Irina Kharina, a former Auschwitz prisoner who is head of a concentration camp prisoners' group and a contact of Pogozhev, took care of his original manuscript, and it was through her that it eventually came to be published in Russian and then in this English translation.

Here, then, is Andrei Pogozhev's personal account of days spent in the Nazis' hellish death camp, of the courage and fortitude of the Soviet POWs, and of his seemingly impossible feat: escape from Auschwitz . . .

This foreword was prepared with the kind assistance of Irina Kharina, former Auschwitz prisoner, Dr Piotr Setkiewicz, Head of Archives State Museum of Auschwitz-Birkenau, Dr Rebecca Wittmann of the University of Toronto, and Ewa Haren.

Artem Drabkin
Christopher Summerville

Maps and Plans

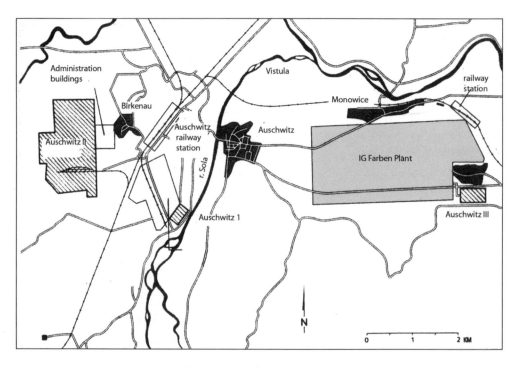

Map of the Auschwitz area, summer 1944

Plan of Auschwitz I

Key

1-28: living barracks (Russian POWs lived in barracks 1–3, 12–14, 22–24)

a: commandant's house

b: main guardhouse

c: commandant's office

d: camp administration

e: hospital

f, g: political prisoners' barracks

h: crematorium

i: guardhouse near camp gates

j: kitchen

k: registration office

l: warehouse for items belonging to the dead prisoners

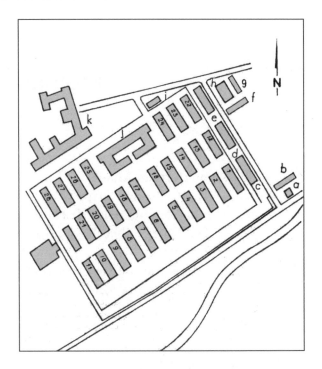

Plan of Auschwitz II

Key

Surviving buildings shown in black

a, b: women's camp

c: main guardhouse ('Death Gates')

d: quarantine camp

e: families' camp

f: Hungarians' camp

g: men's camp

h: gypsies' camp

i: hospital

j, k, o, p: gas chambers

l: memorial

m: warehouse for items belonging to the dead prisoners ('Canada')

n: saunabath

r: buildings under construction ('Mexico')

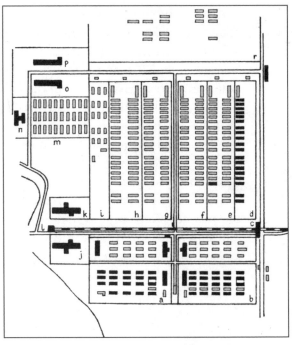

Prologue

FRG, Frankfurt-am-Main

To: The Chairman of the Court in the trial of Auschwitz's Hitlerite criminals, Mr Hans Hofmeyer

To: The Chief Public Prosecutor of the State of Hessen, Mr Fritz Bauer

From: Andrei Alexandrovich Pogozhev (born 1912), a Citizen of the USSR, and former Auschwitz prisoner No. 1418

As an eyewitness to the murder of tens of thousands of people in Auschwitz, I consider it my human duty to fulfil the last will of those victims who perished in terrible anguish.

I offer the Jury and Prosecution my eyewitness testimony regarding the crimes committed against humanity by the accused – Hanz Stark, Stefan Baretzki, Bruno Schlange and Herbert Scherpe – in 1941 and 1942, in the Auschwitz/Oświęcim camp, who were direct participants in the mass murder of prisoners, and who personally killed and tortured inmates. Over the thirteen months of my stay in the camp I was witness to the many hundreds, many thousands, of murders and atrocities committed by these SS men; and for that reason I implore the Jury to call and question me as a witness for the Prosecution.

The crimes I beheld are as yet unknown to history, and so I beg the Jury to accept my testimony – a small fraction of what I saw and suffered – and to punish the SS butchers of Auschwitz. This is a plea from my conscience. The conscience of a man who survived the horrors of Auschwitz.

Andrei Pogozhev

CHAPTER ONE

Entrapment

'Please come in.' I heard a policeman who'd entered the room address me in broken Russian. We walked through a vestibule filled with people of all ages, still hoping to get inside. The policeman courteously opened the door and stepped aside. Left and right, hundreds of eyes were fixed on me. Keeping myself in check, I calmly walked with even stride, down the aisle separating the rows of onlookers, and on to a small desk where Vera, the Interpreter, was sitting. Tense and rigid, she stared at me as I approached, a trace of anxiety in her eyes. But I focused on the Chairman of the Court, whose stony face regarded me with an unblinking beetle-browed stare.

The hall had been built as a place of entertainment, a stage rising above floor level to dominate the scene. Here the Judges and jury sat at a long table, the Chairman in the middle and his two deputies on either side. Along the proscenium were the members of the Public Prosecutor's Office. On the right, by the wall, sat public prosecutors from Frankfurt, East Germany and France. On the left sat the accused with their defence counsel. The rear of the hall was allocated to the public, the dress circle to the Press. But the centre of the chamber was empty, save for the witness stand at which I stopped, saluting the jury with a solemn bow. For some seconds all eyes stared at me: a witness from the Soviet Union, a man who had survived by a miracle, risen from the ashes to tell of days spent in Hell.

The Chairman of the Court spoke and Vera interpreted:
'Surname, forename, patronymic?'
'Pogozhev, Andrei, Alexandrovich.'
'Year of birth?'
'1912.'
'Marital status?'
'Married, two daughters, the older is married and has a daughter . . .'
'Place of residence?'
'The City of Donetsk, in the Ukraine.'
'Current occupation?'
'Mine worker.'
'Do you have any objection to your testimonies being tape-recorded?'
'No.'
'Which religion do you profess?'
'I am an atheist.'
'Will you swear with the cross or without?'
'Without.'
'Raise your right hand.'
The Chairman began speaking German, distinctly enunciating the words and emphasizing some of them. Bewildered, I looked at Vera: 'The words of the oath – to tell the truth only,' she whispered. 'I swear!' I repeated firmly and lowered my hand. The Chairman continued: 'Tell the court how you found yourself in the Auschwitz camp and about your stay there . . .'

The war was both expected and unexpected. People both believed and disbelieved in its possibility: 'There is a non-aggression treaty with the Germans, isn't there?' – 'We trade with Germany and despatch grain, oil and coal there. How can there be a war?' – 'Molotov didn't visit Hitler for nothing. They agreed on peace.' But on that warm, sunny day of 22 June 1941, war struck like a thunderclap.

On 5 July I received a call-up notice, instructing me to report to the *voencomat* [military registration office – trans.] at 9am. On arrival I was told to set my affairs in order within six hours and return at 3pm with my gear. I'd be sent to my unit straight away. I went back home, collected my things, and bade farewell to my mother, wife and daughter. I left home conscious I might never return. My heart was breaking, yet I felt a certain elation: I wanted to participate in the defence of my Motherland. After reporting for duty I found myself among a group of artillery officers herded into the clubroom of some factory, wherein a travelling group of artists gave a variety show: a dose of artificial cheerfulness that was totally out of place. Then we were shepherded onto the troop train.

We got off at Serpukhov. The 252nd Rifle Division was raised here and two artillery regiments formed within it. Next morning several senior officers or 'brass hats' arrived. One of them, a Major, introduced himself as Commander of the 1st Battalion, 787th Artillery Regiment – our new unit. We hurried to prepare our battalion for battle. Everything had to be done within four days because on 10 July the trains would arrive for loading. We knew there was heavy fighting at the front and knocked the battalion together in time for our scheduled departure.

And so, on 10 July 1941 our three batteries were loaded onto a single freight train and we took off. But to our surprise we found ourselves heading towards Moscow. We arrived at Kursk station, then crossed the city along the branch line connecting the capital's Southern and Northern stations, and rolled further onwards towards Kalinin. But somewhere around Lake Seliger, when we were still far away from the front line, the war came upon us unexpectedly.

13th July was a hot day. I was travelling in the officers' carriage – just an ordinary freight wagon – situated at the head of the train. We'd left the carriage door open, passing the time lying on our berths reading. Suddenly there came a tremendous thump followed by a terrible roar. The train screeched to a halt and we darted out of the carriage, rolling down the embankment into a field of rye. Black smoke and white flames were rising from the middle section of the train, and people were spilling from the carriages. A plane with black Swastikas on its wings swooped like a huge carrion crow, strafing us with a hail of lead, before shrieking away out of sight. Some horses, their grooms, and a dozen more men perished in the storm of machine-gun bullets, while many more were wounded. Meanwhile the bomb-blast had torn up the track, leaving rails bent and broken. As for the carriages that caught the explosion, nothing much remained, the passengers having been turned to mincemeat. It was all done in a matter of moments.

Having recovered from the initial shock we began to act. The wounded men were loaded on carts procured in the nearest village and sent to hospital. The dead were buried. An order to unload the train was given: not an easy task in an open field without stationary ramps, but 'zeal can overcome anything' so we managed. The shortage of horses was compensated by trucks and we began our march westwards.

We stopped overnight by the side of a lake. Exhausted, hungry, overwrought, we dropped on the ground and tried to sleep. The night was humid, muggy and hot. Swarms of mosquitoes attacked us, whining and wailing. I never saw such a huge mass of these midges, either before or since. We lay bundled in our greatcoats, suffocating from heat and dripping with sweat. We tried to breathe through our coat-sleeves but the mosquitoes found their way through, filling our mouths and noses. Thus a grotesque night followed a ghastly day.

In the morning we resumed our march and soon our whole division assembled near Lake Seliger. We pitched a temporary camp and began putting ourselves in order. Several days passed in this way.

One night we were awakened by an alarm. We were ordered to be battle-ready and move westward to close with the enemy. A fearful fuss of preparation kicked up but by the morrow every-thing was ready. Gradually the harnessed guns, ammunition wagons, two-wheeled carts, carriages, foot and mounted troops began stretching into marching columns. I galloped up to the head of the column, where the Major (our Battalion Commander) was receiving reports from battery commanders regarding their state of readiness. Unexpectedly, the Major ordered me to stay behind in order to remove the guard posts, after which I was to pick up all remaining gear, load it on carts, and catch up with the regiment. How I disliked the idea of staying while all my comrades were leaving! But I had my orders . . .

The camp was abandoned at dawn, the artillery regiments following the infantry. I began driving around the deserted camp, removing outposts and gathering all those who'd lagged behind into one detachment. Then I ordered all remaining gear, ammo and harness to be loaded up. A reserve gun was hitched to the only motor car, which, occupied by several soldiers and an NCO, I sent speeding after the departed column. Among those who remained under my charge was a starshina [sergeant major – trans.] – a handsome young guy, smart and circumspect, who turned out to be an excellent helper. I almost made the mistake of sending him away with the vehicle but he suggested: 'Comrade Lieutenant, I'd better stay with you. It'll be difficult for you to handle the people and the convoy.' I agreed and kept him with me: a decision I didn't regret.

Thus I suddenly found myself in command of a detachment of some twenty-five soldiers and a convoy. Only the day after the regiment's departure did the Starshina and I manage to collect all the gear, organize the convoy and people, and get them moving. Yet I had no map of the area to serve as a guide, and no idea how long our march would take. We hadn't even been left any rations, and as it was my responsibility to feed the men, I had to buy bread and potatoes at a kolkhoz [collective farm – trans.] we passed on the road. It was fortunate that I had some money on me. Later a herd of cattle came our way, driven by cowherds away from the advancing Germans. I managed to obtain one exhausted calf against a receipt the drovers hoped to exchange for food. At the next halt I tried to get my bearings by consulting one of the locals, an old man, who told me which settlements, forests and rivers lay ahead.

So we were marching west. Refugees – mostly townsfolk with

backpacks and trunks – shuffled towards us. Exhausted, burdened with children, they stopped to sit by the roadside. Some of them warned us to be careful but others yelled: 'Defend our Motherland!' Further to the west saboteurs dressed in Soviet uniform were active. In one village a peasant woman came up and asked us to check on a group of strangers in a neighbouring street. The Starshina and I rode over. A group of men, perhaps ten or eleven in number, were sitting on a log. They were scruffy, poorly dressed, and carried kitbags. The Starshina covered me with his rifle as I rode right up to them: 'Who are you? Present your papers!' – 'We have no papers. We were released from gaol and ordered to go east.' Examining their haggard, emaciated faces, I realized they were not lying and left them alone.

The villages we passed through were half empty. Where were the locals? Maybe these places had been abandoned before the war? After all, collective farmers were unlikely to quit their land and homesteads. Meanwhile we pushed on, our carts groaning under the weight of artillery shells, and our soldiers foot-slogging it under a scorching sun, for only the Starshina and I rode horses.

We were tramping down the street of some half-empty village. I noticed a girl in plain peasant clothes staring at us through the window of a hut. I rode up, asked for a drink, and a moment later she opened the door and handed me a mug of water. But as I drank I couldn't help looking at my benefactress. The mismatch between her looks and mode of dress was striking. She was undoubtedly a city girl: beautiful, refined, with dainty features, but clothed in simple homespun. She, in turn, watched me with a quizzical air: 'Where are you going?' – 'To the front.' – 'What for?' – 'What do you mean, "what for"? To defend the Motherland!' She turned slightly, and motioning towards the gloomy interior of the cabin, asked again: 'To defend *this* existence?' My face froze, but the girl met my gaze and held it. At last I blurted out: 'Do you think the Germans are coming with fire and sword to make our lives better? You are sadly mistaken!' But the maiden muttered: 'I don't know, I don't know . . .' Then, all of a sudden, she ran inside and slammed the door. I placed the mug on the windowsill and galloped after my detachment, which had already disappeared around the corner.

Thus for several days we headed south-west, down the Ostashkov–Peno–Adriapol–Toropets road, then further south towards Staraya Toropa. It was at this point we began meeting casualties coming from the opposite direction. They said our division had been defeated near a place called Il'ino and was in full retreat. But I knew from my experience in the Finnish War [a reference to the 'Winter War' of 1939–40 – trans.] that wounded men frequently exaggerate the horrors of combat, as well as the enemy's numbers, so I paid little attention to these accounts. After a day of such sad encounters and testimonies we stopped at some village and fell asleep, dog tired. In the morning one of my sentries reported that during the night some military unit had passed by in disorder. He'd waited till daylight to make his report because, as he said, he hadn't wished to wake me! At that moment a wounded driver plodded into the hut and confirmed that our division had hastily withdrawn: now there was nothing between us and the Germans but thin air.

Having turned back we soon came across an outpost belonging to our division. At first they wouldn't let us pass, asking us who we were and where we were from. It was just as well they hadn't taken us for the enemy and opened fire. But eventually we made it through, only to find ourselves in a kind of Gypsy camp, with soldiers sleeping around bonfires and wandering in the forest. Some had weapons, some were unarmed, many were wounded and bandaged. With difficulty I found the remnants of my regiment. There in the forest, under a tree, sat the Politruk [political officer – trans.] from our battalion, with no belt and no collar on his blouse. Noticing me, the Politruk – a Tartar – began begging for mercy. It turned out that during the battle he'd feared capture as a political officer and removed the collar of his blouse with its rank insignia, as well as the red stars from his sleeves. Now he was awaiting execution. A soldier was accompanying me and the Politruk pleaded that I should order the man to swap blouses with him. I said I'd no right to do such a thing. I don't know what fate befell the Politruk, but a general atmosphere of menace reigned.

But what had become of the division? We were told it had encountered the enemy's advance guard near Staraya Toropa. Our General should have deployed the division in a transverse front, formed a battle array, sent out reconnaissance patrols, and then advanced or retreated according to circumstances – elementary stuff. But having learned the Germans in his front were pulling back, the General immediately followed. Abandoning the rule book to seize – as he thought – a priceless opportunity, the General ordered: 'Pursue the enemy and destroy him!' And so the division set off along the forest road in marching columns. Meanwhile, the main German force was waiting, having peeled off the high road into the forest. When the division approached Il'ino the Germans struck from both flanks and a massacre began. Along with a considerable number of commanders and soldiers, a great haul of weapons and equipment was lost in the subsequent rout. The division – recently formed from reservists – was already a wreck. All that remained was this Gypsy camp, scattered about the forest, which, as we discovered, was encircled by the enemy.

Discipline, too, was a casualty. No one was in the mood for orders, so all authority was undermined. And the situation was exacerbated by hunger, for the supply train had been lost during the battle and no food had been organized. In these conditions criminal elements surfaced and a binge of thieving broke out. My trunk – containing all my gear, spare outfit, underwear, footwear, and so on – was among the items that 'disappeared'. I counted myself lucky I still had the stuff in my saddle-bags, but they were soon cleaned out by scoundrels – even my trench coat, which had been strapped to the saddle, was stolen. Thus I was left with clothes on my back and my map case, in which I kept shaving kit, soap, towel, paper and pencil. Thankfully my documents and photographs were still safe in the pockets of my blouse. And I still had some money, which I used to buy a greatcoat and backpack from some starshina. Finally I found an abandoned mess tin, minus its spoon: but it didn't matter, as there was nothing to eat anyway.

This grievous situation couldn't continue much longer. Had the

Germans known our condition, they could've finished us off with minor forces. And so we middle-ranking officers, the lieutenants, began raising our voices in an attempt to restore order. Almost spontaneously, and of its own accord, a detachment of commanders coalesced and organized a defence line near the edge of the forest. We were headed by some infantry captain or major.

There was a small clearing in front of us, and beyond it, where the forest began again, the Germans had set up a machine-gun post. We had no tools to dig trenches and were armed, for the most part, with pistols. Furthermore, ammunition was short and no medical help was available. Somehow we managed to scavenge some food, and when the shooting began we bandaged the wounded ourselves with our own field dressings. The Germans frequently opened up with their machine- and submachine-guns but we returned almost no fire. This, it seems, only made the Germans nervous, especially at night, for they constantly fired flares over no-man's land.

> In its fall the rocket shone
> As a star does when it dies.
> If that sight once meets your eyes
> The memory will ne'er be gone.

Yes, it's impossible to forget those days and nights . . .

We expected that, having set up a defence line – that is, provided some safety for the camp – we'd give the brass hats chance to organize the soldiers wandering in the forest into disciplined infantry units, but it never happened. Soon the enemy began squeezing the perimeter: now only small bands of fugitives could escape, which basically meant 'every man for himself'. Some officers had already disappeared, so we took off northwards through the forest, for the roads and villages were crawling with Germans. If we came upon an enemy patrol, we'd work around it with a few shots. In one spot, as we were crossing from one forest to another, a German tank blocked our way and opened up with its cannon. We pulled back to some ravine, slept in the forest, and continued our march next morning.

Once we were passing a hospital while it was being evacuated. Lots of badly wounded men lay in rows on the bare grass, with two or three nurses bustling around them. Seeing us pass, the invalids cursed us for supposedly leaving them to be slaughtered by the Germans. We replied that we were trying to break out of the encirclement, as much for their sakes as our own, but the broken, bandaged men wouldn't believe us and kept up a tirade of abuse. Our situation was difficult, but the lot of those unlucky casualties was much worse: at least we were on our feet and with weapons in our hands, while they lay helpless, half-dead, unable to influence their own fate. Meanwhile, some enemy detachment began dogging our trail, catching up with us in the forest. We had to turn around, stretch into a file, lie on the ground, and return fire with our pistols and rifles. The Germans were audacious, however, and sent a submachine-gunner into our rear. But when he began spraying us with bullets from behind we about-faced, fired a salvo, and successfully silenced him, for he soon disappeared.

During our wanderings in search of a 'window' through which to escape, we reached the forest edge: here the enemy-occupied village of Vorob'y could be seen. It was at this point we encountered a group from one of our rifle regiments, led by several officers. An overbearing captain acted as battalion commander and invited me (and a fellow officer) for a meeting. The Captain announced that he'd studied the situation: there was a small German blockhouse in the village, but if we could push past we'd break out of the encirclement. To achieve this the Captain suggested we unite our groups, concentrate in front of the village before dark, and on his signal dash forward shooting and yelling. He said the Germans usually slept at night, so the strike would be unexpected, while ravines and bushes would conceal our approach.

Dusk fell. We gathered our soldiers, explained the task, and advanced on the village as directed by the Captain. We were in high spirits, marching with enthusiasm in the belief we'd smash the Germans with our sudden strike and break free by morning.

And yet the Captain deployed two sergeants to wave us on with weapons, demanding we move more quickly. The reason for this insult was not clear, as we were proceeding with all speed and needed no urging.

Having reached the village we hid and waited for the Captain's signal, our nerves stretched to the limit. Suddenly I heard a command from the enemy's side: the Germans were not sleeping but preparing to meet us! And still we waited – but the signal never came. At last the spell was broken when a soldier's spirit failed and he let out a scream: 'Hurrah!' Everyone jumped up, joined in the shouting, and rushed forward firing. At that moment a white flare burst overhead, lighting up everything around. Next came the roaring blast of machine-gun fire, as a glut of glowing tracers flashed towards us. At first I yelled 'Hurrah!' with the rest and ran forward, but dazzled by the firing I stumbled and smacked into the ground. Maybe this fall saved me, for the fire was close-range, nearly point-blank. Everything blurred: flashes, shouts, shots and darkness. Already the attack had stalled and those in advance began pulling back. But I remained pinned to the ground by a swarm of blazing bullets, scratching the earth with my nails in search of salvation. I was whispering something over and over, some kind of incantation that would save me . . .

When the firing slackened I rose a little, but saw only dead bodies. Some German spotted me, for a solitary shot rang out, the bullet whizzing past my head. Somehow I managed to crawl to the nearest ravine – dogged by recurring shots – and then back to the forest. There I came across some fellow survivors of the Captain's strike. But the Captain and his officers were nowhere to be seen. It became clear from talks with the riflemen that the Captain and his cronies had been hanging around here for days, organizing 'breakouts' with arriving groups but never taking part themselves. On this occasion – having 'studied the situation' – the Captain had decided to use us for a demonstrational strike that would force the Germans to concentrate their fire, allowing him and his co-conspirators to edge around the village and break out of the encirclement. Moreover, he had deliberately directed us onto the centre of the German defence, knowing very well there would be great slaughter.

And so we retreated deeper into the forest, having lost so many people in this night attack. Next day we joined another group of infantrymen in an attempt to break through near the village of Romanovo. Again, nothing came of it – except further losses – so we rolled back into the forest, making our way north-east in small groups.

The situation had become desperate, for we had grown weak with hunger. Sometimes we found mushrooms, which we boiled without salt in our mess tins. Otherwise we chewed flax seeds and oil-cake from our pockets – although this stuff soon ran out. Once we came across the hide of some animal, probably a goat, and tore it to pieces, sucking its sour, inner side. Then, stumbling in the grass, I discovered the nest of some bird, which fluttered out from under my feet. Two small, spotted eggs lay in the nest: I boiled them in the mess tin and gobbled them greedily.

Initially the Germans rarely made forays into the forests, preferring to occupy the villages and roads. But eventually they began combing the woods, patrolling the footpaths in files, led by a soldier dressed in Soviet uniform. This man would keep a look-out for wandering fugitives, whom he would beckon over. Thinking the 'Soviet' was on their side, our men would approach, whereupon German troops appeared with submachine-guns, yelling: 'Rus, surrender!' Any man who failed to put up his hands was immediately shot point-blank. Thus the criss-crossing paths were beaten down in all directions, as people rushed around the forest looking for a way out, only to find death or captivity. But the bullets that claimed so many lives were not only German: some men were killed by comrades for a crumb of bread. I remember one corpse lying in a glade. The dead man lay on his back, apparently staring up at the clear blue sky, but worms were already writhing in his wide-open eyes. As for me, I saw only hopelessness. There was no way out. But I still had bullets in my pistol – suicide? I didn't want to die. Besides, three other lives were under my care, men who looked at me with hope.

On 15 August 1941 (I well remember this accursed day) we came across a group of peasants in the forest and asked them for food. We were dying of hunger but the peasants gave us nothing, telling us that food from looted stores could be found at a nearby village, which, they added, was free of Germans.

We found the place, before which stood a solitary house and shed. We knew the Germans would place outposts around an occupied village, so we watched for a long while from the safety of the forest. No guard post was in sight. Finally, one of my soldiers crept along a fence to the first house, in order to take a closer look. When he reported the house empty, we carefully headed towards the village. But as soon as we passed that first house, which we thought unoccupied, German soldiers dashed out shouting and shooting from submachine-guns, cutting us off from the forest. We were caught in a trap.

I'd managed to fire a shot from my pistol when one of my soldiers grabbed my hand with a yell: 'Don't shoot, they'll kill us!' The Germans pounced on me and began beating me with rifle butts, knocking the pistol from my hand, felling me to the ground and kicking me with iron-shod jackboots. I was wearing a soldier's greatcoat over my officer's uniform and in the scuffle it was torn open. Straight away the Germans saw my uniform: the waist- and shoulder-belts with shining buckles, the officer's cubes on my collar badges, the yellow leather map case. They stopped beating me and began to look me over: 'Du bist Kommissar?' ('Are you a Kommissar?') I barely managed to answer: 'Nein.' But the Germans kept looking, bending over me as I lay on the ground, indifferent to my fate. Dragging me to my feet they marched me off, shoving me in the back with a rifle butt. Weakened by hunger and the beating I shuffled along in a daze, as if caught in another man's dream. For it seemed to me that I no longer existed, that I was lying lifeless at the entrance to the village and they were escorting someone else . . .

CHAPTER TWO

Stalag 308

The committee of investigation into Hitlerite crimes in Poland has finished examining the case of the former Nazi POW camps and Żagań mass graves of the Second World War period, discovered near Żagań, in the territory of the Zelenogurskoye Voevodstvo (Province) of Poland.

On the basis of scrupulous study of data collected during the investigation, including testimony from fifty witnesses, it has been established that during the Second World War, near the town of Żagań (formerly called in German Sagan), there were several POW camps with branches in Święntoszów (Neuhammer) and Konin-Żagański (Kanau). Initially there were Polish POWs in these camps, then Belgian, English, French, Yugoslav and Soviet. Stalag 308 contained Soviet citizens exclusively. As the Polish Agency of Press (PAP) reports, 100,000 POWs were processed in each of the camps.

The investigation has shown that treatment of these POWs was an unprecedented breach of international law. Treatment of the Soviet POWs was especially atrocious: they were starved to death, tormented, tortured, murdered. A considerable number of mass and single graves were discovered near the camps, some of which contained the bodies of POWs. The location of the graves was revealed on the basis of witnesses' testimonies and official German documents, as well as material evidence – insignia of military personnel from specific countries, remnants of uniforms, buttons etc. Excavation of the graves was accompanied by great difficulties, for the Hitlerites had planted woods over them.

The facts revealed during the investigation testify to the Hitlerites' criminal treatment of POWs and unparalleled flouting of international law. The behaviour of the Fascists towards the Soviet POWs bore signs of genocide. As PAP reports, the unveiling of a monument to the victims of Hitlerite barbarism will take place in the grounds of the former camp at Żagań on 3 September.

From 'The Secret of the Żagań Forests' – a TASS report, quoted in the *Sotsialisticheski Donbass* (*Donbass Socialist*) newspaper, Wednesday, 28 August 1968.

The second half of September 1941. A flat area of sandy ground was fenced with barbed wire in the middle of a thick, age-old forest. The wind swayed the tops of giant trees, caressing them with soothing whispers, but down on the ground its presence was never felt. Here swarms of stirring bodies gave out a discordant buzz, which, reverberating round the trees, rose up and dissolved in the blue sky. Before the only gate stood rows of barbed-wire cages 2x2 metres in size. These were punishment cells and they were always full. Those inmates who still possessed some strength stood upright, though unsteadily, shifting from foot to foot. Most lay curled up, with shoulder-blades sticking out. Thousands of Soviet POWs – alone or in groups – aimlessly plodded about. The variety of uniforms resembled a trade fair motley: blouses, shirts, civilian suits, raincoats, trench coats, overcoats. Dirty unshaven faces on the verge of starvation. Fevered eyes, twisted mouths . . .

It was warm in the daytime – if the weather was good – but the nights were terrible: no salvation from the icy cold. The only construction inside the enclosure was the concrete ablution block, which gave shelter from the chill for a few dozen. Places had to be got during the day, and those who pushed their way inside slept standing upright, warming each other: it was impossible to fall because of the overcrowding – but to fall meant certain death.

Outside the bitter cold compelled people to scratch into the sandy soil with their bare hands. In twos and threes men would scrape shallow holes in which to huddle, covered – if they were lucky – by an overcoat. Thus hundreds of holes appeared each day, which frequently became graves for those who failed to clamber out when the mad crowd stampeded. For the camp administration amused itself by having guards throw turnips over the fence into the crowd, close to those places where a large number of shelters had been dug. Thousands of men, out of their minds with hunger, would rush about, pouncing on the turnips, trampling underfoot those trapped in their burrows. The scenes of these mad scrambles were easily identified afterwards: flattened patches of earth with hands, feet and torsos sticking out. But despite the permanent danger of being buried alive, the cold made people dig new shelters, which became fresh graves a few days later.

The deliberate and cold-blooded tormenting of Soviet POWs with cold, hunger and various sadistic tortures was conducted systematically and on a daily basis. By taking all possible precautions one could protect oneself from provocations, but there was no salvation from cold and hunger. Nor there was any hope of an improvement in our situation. Every new day sapped one's strength, and it was strange to look at one's comrades, as rumours of cannibalism began to spread. Something had to be ventured, otherwise certain death was in store.

Ten of us decided to dig a tunnel under the barbed wire. Of this group I well remember the following comrades: Souslov, a Russian mechanic from the TsAGI [Central Institute of Hydrodynamics – trans.]; Andrei, a lively man from Donbass; and Pavlik Sten'kin, who was almost a boy. Later I will speak of their fates.

A place for the tunnel was chosen at the spot where the forest came almost right up against the fence. We began digging by hand, in-between flashes from flares, which the guards fired every thirty minutes. After two nights we'd dug a 5-metre passage, which extended 1 metre beyond the perimeter fence. Having cleared the wire we hoped to push on quickly, as we wouldn't have to disguise the hole from above. Two nights of nervous and physical strain went by like none before. We felt neither hunger nor cold. Everyone was animated. A dangerous moment came when a security patrol paced in front of the tunnel at the precise moment a flare went up, illuminating everything. And yet, unbelievably, all passed off safely.

But at noon the next day guards burst into the camp, armed with rifles and batons, and proceeded to separate several hundred Russians from the masses in the vicinity of the tunnel. Some officers appeared. The tunnel had been found by accident when it caved in near the fence; now soldiers were busy backfilling it. One of the officers barked: 'Who did it?' Silence. 'Whoever points them out gets to work in the kitchen!' Silence. 'If they are not given up in five minutes those who did it will be shot!' A chorus of coughing and moaning resounded. They drove us towards the open gate, past the wire cages where 'offenders' lived out their last hours. The end? Maybe that would be better? My feet were impossibly heavy. I'm sure that, had I been alone, I would have lacked the courage to lift them: but it's not so frightening to meet death with one's comrades. Despite physical weakness my mind was not stupefied with fear. My rapid thoughts were clear and logical. I felt bitterness in the depths of my soul for the last months, and pangs of guilt for the Motherland.

We spent the next two hours waiting to be shot. We stood in a clearing next to a railway line, the camp out of sight behind a wall of forest trees. We'd got used to the idea of our impending death as the logical culmination of our inhumane treatment. A submachine-gun stuttered somewhere in the forest: for the comrades who remained in the camp we were no longer alive.

Before nightfall a freight train stopped in front of us. To our great surprise they pushed us into a truck, counting heads. As soon as the doors closed everyone began talking at once. Loud jokes and laughter – we were ready to sing for joy! All were of one mind: wherever we were being taken, at least we would not return to the camp.

CHAPTER THREE

Auschwitz

Early morning, 7 October 1941. With a clanging of buffers the train stopped. Almost immediately a creaking and a rumbling approached our truck at regular intervals: someone on the outside was unbolting the doors with a practised jolt. Our door opened and darkness breathed cool air on our faces. Silently, shapeless shadows began tumbling out of the trucks. Wobbling on shaky legs, men tottered from the train: those who fell rolled aside to avoid being trampled. Men were swinging their arms, bending their legs, bowing, trying to revive deadened limbs. All greedily gulped fresh air saturated with moisture. The effect was intoxicating: my head was swimming, so I stood in silence for a few seconds with eyes shut. Sensing the approach of dawn I lifted my eyelids: buildings and a web of fences were emerging from the gloom. Everything was coming to life.

The train had stopped before a T-shaped area, fenced with double rows of barbed wire some 3 metres high. The upper bar of the 'T' ran alongside the platform, twin gates at each end letting trains in and out. A small brick shack stood at its centre. Meanwhile, the stem of the 'T' stretched away into darkness.

As daylight increased we saw curious creatures 500 metres away behind the barbed wire – people in striped suits. This was an unexpected sight: memories from books and movies told us that convicts wore striped suits; but the beautiful two-storey buildings didn't correspond to our notion of penal servitude. We wanted to believe we'd left the worst behind in the Żagań forest and had counted ourselves lucky, thinking our new situation couldn't be worse than back there. What naivety!

A guard with a submachine-gun opened the gates: about two dozen inmates in striped clothes entered the square, clattering loudly with their wooden clogs, and carrying small cases and stools. They were accompanied by a soldier armed with what looked like a whip, about 1 metre in length. This group was followed by an officer, a very young man, who, perhaps on account of his extreme youth, had adopted a theatrically cocky bearing. He puffed out his flat chest, flung his head back, and looked around with obvious contempt, while constantly adjusting the kid gloves on his boyish hands. Our eyes caught sight of the silver skull and crossbones on his collar. This emblem of death – familiar to us from the masts of high-voltage power-supply lines – emanated a horrid chill.

With open curiosity we scrutinized the arriving inmates, who paid us no attention at all as they hastily set out stools against the wall of the shack. Most were Jews. Their appearance shocked us. They looked pathetic and helpless in their comical, crumpled, convict suits, so baggy and dirty. But on their skinny, emaciated faces, only one expression was visible: fear. They even feared to look at us. When the stools were set out and the cases opened, one of the inmates loudly announced in broken Russian: 'Come and get your hair cut. We won't tell you twice!' – 'Ja, ja, schnell!' yelled the soldier, cracking his whip. His spiteful stare, twitching knots of muscles under clean-shaven cheeks, and body tilted forward as if for a leap, all left no doubt he was ready to use the whip at any time. His whole figure was so brutish that all those standing alongside backed off. And so the haircut commenced.

The barbers wouldn't answer our questions, as if they couldn't understand the language or were deaf. My countryman, Andrei Shkryl, from the village of Mandrykino in the Donetskaya Oblast province, sat down to have his hair cut. Before the war he'd worked as a projectionist somewhere in the Western Ukraine, so he knew a little Polish. He began quietly repeating the same questions in Ukrainian and Polish to the barber working on him: 'Please tell us where we are. Which town is this?' I stood next to the barber and saw how uneasily he glanced at the SS-Mann, and how his hands were trembling. One could guess immediately by his twitchy face that he understood Andrei's questions, and would like to answer, but was afraid. At last, seizing a moment when the soldier turned away to speak to a guard behind the wire, the barber hissed a mixture of Polish, Russian and German words: 'This is Poland. The town of Auschwitz. A terrible camp. Beware of the SS-Mann, he understands Russian.'

After some time the eldest of the barbers – the one who had announced the haircut – stood on a stool at the command of the SS-Mann with the whip and declared: 'All of you will be escorted into the camp by hundreds. Strip yourself naked. Clothes into the shed. Take nothing with you. Before the line up in front of those gates everyone will have to dip his head into disinfectant fluid. You'll get food and bedding in the camp. Understood?'

The mention of food raised everyone's spirits. We crowded next to the shed with exclamations and jokes. Those who had had their hair cut began to strip off. Even the most exhausted began to show signs of life.

Is it possible to convey in words the condition of people reduced to desperation by hunger and thirst? No, it's impossible. It's hard to endure hunger, but to endure thirst is incomparably harder and more painful. And what had been happening in the truck? People had been losing consciousness from the stifling air, which only amplified thirst. Dry, cracked lips begged for only one thing: water. Those who were in the worst condition, on the brink of madness, were moved by their mates closer to the bars of the windows, to the fresh air: a difficult feat in trucks crammed to the limit. When it was completely intolerable they were offered the only thing available – cooled urine. But all that was behind us . . .

The first of our naked comrades came out of the shack. My God, the look of them! Their clothes had been hiding everything, but now their thin arms, legs, necks, sharp shoulder-blades, ribs sticking out over sunken bellies, were appalling. Only the will and the craving to live were making them move, making their hearts beat and warming their bodies.

An argument broke out among those crowding around a concrete vessel, resembling a drum, dug into the ground. There was greenish water in it. Nobody believed this smelly fluid was for disinfection and nobody wanted to be submerged in it. An SS-Mann quickly strode up: 'What is happening here?' he asked. A dense wall of naked bodies stood before him. Everyone was looking at the soldier expectantly. Sensing his power and superiority the SS-Mann roared: 'Good it is! Dip in!' Suddenly his glare fell on the right hand of a tall guy nearby, which was carefully holding a photograph so as not to crumple it. 'What's that?' hissed the SS-Mann, 'did you hear? No take anything! Did you hear?!' – 'It's my daughter's photo. Do you understand? She's so high . . .' Smiling shyly, the guy showed the child's height with the hand that was holding the photo. A smart crack of the whip and the photo fell to the ground: we could see the image of a wide-eyed girl, a splendid bow in her hair. Her father bent down to pick up the photo but a lash of the whip got him upright straight away. The SS-Mann stepped forward and with unhidden spite trod on the photo, then smeared it in the mud like a gob of spit. And then an unexpected thing happened. The soldier hadn't even taken his boot off the photo when a heavy blow on his ear knocked him off his feet. His field cap fell into the disinfectant and he nearly followed it. Then the officer leaped up with his pistol drawn: 'Shoot, you scum! Shoot!' That proud father was the first of our comrades to die in Auschwitz. We knew he'd made a stupid move, but in our hearts we couldn't blame him.

Soldiers and officers ran up to the sounds of shots, raising a hue-and-cry. Unintelligible orders tore our ears. Whips cracked and whistled. There was a queue before the vessel. Those who'd undergone 'disinfection' squatted in rows of five men each, in front of the gates, blue and shivering from cold, pain, and resentment. The gates opened. The first hundred ran through, flanked by soldiers with whips. I ran with the second or third hundred.

After some 500 metres we stopped for several minutes before a concrete fence and another set of barbed-wire gates. Then we were counted off and the gates opened. We ran again. My head was spinning and my whole body shivered with cold.

We were inside a large block enclosed by two-storey buildings. The cleanliness was amazing. We came across soldiers and officers with the same grisly emblem on their collar badges. Here and there we spotted prisoners in striped suits: when they looked our way they'd try to avoid us. Around the corner of one of the houses we found ourselves in a large concreted area. The ground was almost entirely covered by a system of pipes with shower outlets, from which water spurted, creating a fine mist. A voice resounded from somewhere: 'Wash and bath!' The water pressure was powerful, and where the spurts hit my body I felt acute pain.

Prisoners in striped outfits, shaved and well fed, were in charge here. Their suits did not hang like sacks and were not filthy and crumpled like those of the barbers. They were fitted to height and build, clean and ironed. And their behaviour towards the SS men was completely different to that of the barbers. These men spoke to the SS guards almost as equals, laughing and joking. The bands on their left arms carried bright inscriptions we couldn't yet understand: 'Kapo' and 'Blockältester' ['Kapo' was the term for a prisoner acting as an overseer; and 'Blockältester' – more correctly 'Blockälteste' – meant 'block elder' or 'block supervisor' – trans.]

In the evening sharp whistles resounded throughout the camp: the signal for 'Appell' – the mandatory daily roll-call. Inmates with armbands squared us up into rows with fists and sticks. But our minds refused to think, or our bodies to move. Many were unable to remain in line and collapsed on the ground in front of the swaying ranks.

After roll-call they began moving us into houses or 'blocks'. As each man entered he was thrown an old cotton blanket, then a tin containing 800 grammes of soup was thrust into his trembling hands. By now we were only dimly aware of what was happening to us, as if walking through a fog . . .

CHAPTER FOUR

Extermination

Our first days in Auschwitz dumbfounded us. They transformed us from individual human beings into a herd of animals. For no clear reason they would stampede us for roll-call, the issue of meagre camp rations, examinations, or whatever else, speeding us along with the loathsome word 'Los!' All the time our drovers cracked their whips in the air – or on our backs and heads – depending on their mood. These monsters were attached to us as 'interpreters' but were recruited from the criminal classes of every nation. They were particularly zealous when observed by the camp administration: we could tell by their behaviour when SS men were around.

Everyone had to be present for roll-call. Sick men unable to move – even dead men still listed as living – would be brought out from the blocks. Roll-call lasted about two hours. Consequently, columns of naked Soviet POWs would stagger into line and stand the whole time, the sick and the dead stretched out on the concrete before them. During the course of roll-call the numbers of sick and dead increased as more men collapsed and fell out of line. During the first days my countryman, Andrei Shkryl, reached his limit. His weak health, undermined by starvation and the cold shower of the first day, finally broke down. Having no strength to stand in the column he wept soundlessly in our arms as long as we could hold him up. A day later he was no more.

No wind, no rain, no bitter cold could interrupt the established order. So it went, day by day, through October and the first half of November. Meanwhile, the SS guards and the camp aristocracy were already dressed for winter – they even wore oval-shaped cloth ear-flaps against the cold. But we still stood stripped to the skin. Secretly, however, I and many others managed to tie thin wooden tiles to our feet, which offered some protection from the cold concrete of the square or 'Appellplatz'. And so we'd stamp on the spot, warming ourselves with the breath and heat of our bodies . . .

At last the long-awaited 'Achtung!' would sound and the SS supervisor would appear, accompanied by a Blockältester, a criminal inmate and one of the pillars of the camp aristocracy. After the headcount we remained in our places while the dead – with those who'd simply lost consciousness mixed in – were brought out to be sent to the crematorium. Everyone was supposed to return to the blocks they'd been initially allotted. Those unable to move were returned first, followed by the sick and crippled. Only then were the remainder dismissed. The interpreters – loyal hounds of the Blockältesters – stood by each block, vigilantly tallying the incomers.

My block was kind of a dormitory. A central corridor ran down its whole length with rooms on both sides. One of the corner rooms served as both latrine and mortuary. It was strictly forbidden to move from one room to another – you couldn't even visit even a dying comrade. Free access to the latrine was granted, however, but one had to run there and back. Thus the corridor, for the most part, remained empty. As for the rooms, each one had a stove in the middle, faced with iron. Bunk beds of bare planks crammed the remaining space, stacked three high, with perhaps a metre between each row.

Rations were issued room by room. In order to receive food, inmates had to step out of the room and into the corridor one at a time. An interpreter doled out the rations while another, armed with a whip, ensured that proper respect was paid to their persons and 'work'. Then, in silence, each man returned: no comments, no objections. In the morning we received half a litre of warm fluid, lacking definite colour or smell, which went by the name of 'tea'. In the afternoon we received 800 grammes of something resembling beetroot soup, containing perhaps a hint of cereal, potatoes and sometimes meat. In the evening we received a brick-shaped loaf to be shared between six men. This was supplemented by a sliver of margarine and a dab of jam or some fishy-smelling cheese. Dividing the bread into six equal portions was up to us, so the task always went to a trustworthy man.

Our Blockältester was a young, rosy-cheeked German rogue named Rudolph. He rarely beat Russians himself, but when he did, it was with relish. Normally Rudolf preferred to beat the interpreters for not sufficiently thrashing the Russians. But Rudolf rarely beat anyone – either Russians or interpreters – without putting on a pair of neat kid gloves, which he carried at all times. Meanwhile a barber, specially attached to him, massaged Rudolf's whole body every day, rubbing it with aromatic oils. On account of these peculiarities the Blockältester was dubbed 'the Toff'.

Rudolf the Toff was endowed with an uncommon musical gift: he loved to whistle. Indeed, the variety of tunes the Toff could whistle was truly staggering. He even performed Russian folk-songs, keeping us all spellbound. But we soon learned to use this love of whistling as a means of self-defence. For example, the Toff's whistling informed us of his approach and indicated what kind of mood he was in. A lack of whistling warned us to be careful.

The Toff never took part in food distribution, regarding it beneath his dignity. But with his consent the interpreters always fished out of their soup drums the most edible morsels for the Toff, his dog and his cronies. In short, our Blockältester was a scoundrel with the subtle manners of an aristocrat. We didn't know – and couldn't imagine – what crime had landed him in the camp, but one thing was clear: the Toff was an out-and-out sadist and butcher. He and an SS buddy, nicknamed the 'White Hare', took pleasure in organizing savage punishments, each trying to outdo the other in cruelty.

Thus life – with its triumphs, troubles, joys and cares – went on somewhere far away from us. Meanwhile, we found ourselves cast overboard, crippled in our souls, drowning in a sea of suffering and humiliation. Over the distant horizon our comrades and kinfolk were carrying on a fierce and bloody crusade against the dark evil that threatened life, love and Motherland. But we had infamously quit this holy war and were unable to help. We were no longer sure even as to its direction. And yet rumours would reach us on mysterious wings. Arriving in unknown ways, who could tell the twisted, tortuous path they'd taken to reach us? Understanding how they must have been distorted en route, how much nonsense they must have absorbed, we tried to view them critically. And yet, just as there's no smoke without fire, a rumour must retain the seed of truth from which it blossomed. Pondering these rumours permitted us to hazard some conclusions. And our conclusions imbued us with faith and hope.

The stupefaction of the first days was leaving us. We instinctively began assessing the situation and adapting our behaviour to preserve our already fragile health. But we were hampered in this by our lack of knowledge regarding the camp class system, for significant divisions separated the inmates. At the top of the heap were those who enjoyed the confidence of the camp authorities, from whom they received certain privileges: the so-called 'aristocracy'. At the bottom were those who, like us, received no favours and feared for their very lives. But in between the two extremes existed a vulnerable 'bourgeoisie'. Terrified of slipping into the mass of ordinary men, whose fate was wholly dependent on the will of chance, these toads would do anything to ingratiate themselves with those higher on the ladder. Thus they constituted the most dangerous class of all, and from this scum the interpreters were recruited.

Suddenly a new interpreter appeared. His general behaviour was not much different from his fellows, but instead of yelling in German or camp jargon, he spoke pure native Russian. We were surprised when, one afternoon, he strode into our room and stood at the window, silently glancing at us from time to time. He was a slender man – despite being middle-aged – and in his dark hair were strong streaks of grey. His striped jacket and trousers were fitted, and his boots were polished to a glitter. A green triangle was sewn on the left breast of his jacket, and next to it was a number on a white strip. His face, with its frowning gaze, was skinny and neatly shaved. Everyone in the room fell silent. A moment later he broke the spell: 'I'm a Russian too, actually. Yes, a Russian by descent. But this is the first time I've seen so many Russians together.' He spoke slowly, quietly, not looking at anyone. His eyes were fixed on the window and his face didn't change expression at all. Suddenly he made a sharp turn and walked out. We heard loud talking in the corridor – someone was swearing – and then all was quiet.

We looked at each other in amazement. Then someone hissed: 'He's a Belogvardeyets [a White Guardsman – member of the anti-Bolshevik forces during the Russian Civil War of 1918–22 – trans.] if anything. How d'you like that? A Russian's turned up! That's a smack in the face!' – 'Don't you get us in trouble!' came a sharp reply. At that moment the Russian returned, taking post by the window once more: 'You've been brought here for extermination,' he said. 'There's only one way out of here – the crematorium. This is a death camp.' – 'But you're still alive, aren't you?' – 'Some of you will survive too.' – 'What should we do? What *can* we do?' – 'Keep your eyes open. Do your best. I can do nothing to help. It's not up to us . . .'

He told us his surname – Skorobogatov. He'd been born in Russia but lived all his life in Poland. It turned out that he came to our room to spy out of the window, to be ready for any encounter. During one of Skorobogatov's visits someone asked him: 'Tell me, what kind of rank is Blockführer?'

'Blockführer is an SS rank. The word means "block leader" and he is responsible for the number of inmates in a block. The Blockältester answers to the Blockführer. He's one who's already gained favour with the higher-ups and is usually a German. And, well, we interpreters are the Blockältester's assistants.'

'So, are you nominated or do you volunteer?'

'At roll-call they asked: "Those who know Russian, step forward." Of course, I didn't have to admit I knew Russian, but wanted to get more familiar with it.'

'And who's the one who took our Pyotr for himself – the one who knows English? He wears a black jacket with a yellow armband on the left sleeve.'

'That's Bruno, a camp Kapo. He's got a number one. Remember that Kapos are work supervisors and pose the greatest danger to prisoners' lives. They have a privileged position. They are judge, jury and executioner in work teams. Stay away from them, just in case.'

'Why do the Blockführers and all the soldiers wear death's head collar badges?'

'This is the emblem of the SS Totenkopf division. They're élite troops and the mainstay of the Gestapo. There are no simple soldiers among them.'

'What does the green of the triangle on your chest mean?'

'If someone has a red triangle it means he was sentenced on political charges; green – criminal ones; black – sabotage. The letter in the triangle shows your nationality. I've got a Roman "P", which means Polish.'

'How long have you been here?'

'About a year.'

'We saw Soviet flags and belts in a shed at the train station. Were there any Russians before us?'

'I don't know. I haven't seen any . . .'

'How many Russians are in the camp now?'

'Don't know for sure – maybe 20,000.'

'Who else is in the camp apart from Russians?'

'Mostly Poles and Jews. There are some Czechs, Slovaks. And a few Germans.'

'Is it possible to escape from here?'

Skorobogatov glanced at the questioner and grinned: 'People say anything that is not impossible is possible. But in this case even the possible is almost impossible! I know of no successful escape from the camp. You may have noticed that around the camp are two rows of concrete posts with barbed wire attached to insulators. The barbed wire on each post is fixed on both sides in a checkerboard pattern. The space between the wires is about 20 centimetres. The wire is always switched to high voltage. To touch it means death. On the outer side of the barbed-wire fence there's a solid concrete wall about 3 metres high. Five metres from the inner side – a warning wire. Whoever approaches it or steps over it will be shot dead by guards on the watch towers or any nearby SS-Mann. They'll kill you and be rewarded for averting an attempt to escape. Is it clear? Now judge for yourself if it's possible to escape.'

A few days later Skorobogatov disappeared as suddenly as he'd appeared. The day before his departure a new Blockführer was appointed to our block: none other than the Toff's playmate known as 'the White Hare'. This man was a sadistic SS bully, well known for his brutality during roll-calls. When Skorobogatov discovered our block had been given over to the White Hare, he warned us: 'Brace yourselves! Now you'll have no rest by night or day. He's a dog among dogs.' According to Skorobogatov, the White Hare – otherwise known as Stefan Baretzki – was a Polish German. He'd been on the Russian front and had narrowly survived death there. He didn't regard Poles, Czechs, Yugoslavs – let alone Jews – as people. He particularly hated the Soviets.

On the very first day of the White Hare's reign we saw how right Skorobogatov was: the darkest days had come. Prior to the White Hare's arrival we'd been beaten by the interpreters and finished off by starvation, cold, and disease. But now circumstances changed for the worse. For the White Hare found fun and pleasure in torment, torture and murder. He behaved like a brute and made others do the same. Before his arrival there was relative calm between roll-calls, when exhausted bodies could relax a while; but after the White Hare's advent our nerves remained under constant strain, jangled by the sudden sound of screams in the corridor, the slamming of doors, and the stamping of feet.

The Russian contingent was already thinning, and the number

of our comrades lying on the ground or sitting by the walls at roll-call – certain candidates for the crematorium – was growing daily. Meanwhile, men busied themselves, each in his own way. Some lay silently, others talked endlessly on the most varied topics. They mostly recalled the past and rarely dreamed about the future. But all were tormented by one thought: what was going to happen to us? We didn't want to believe the horrible reality. Is an excruciating death inevitable? Our comrades were dying on the bunks next to us – some quietly, some in delirium – and we couldn't help them or even express our commiseration. We didn't want to believe in this nightmare.

My friend from the days of Stalag 308, Souslov, with whom I had made the tunnel, often lost control when speaking about our fate. A tall man, big-boned, usually unhurried and sober-minded, he'd change during our discussions. Our situation was maddening him beyond measure: 'We're fools! Fools and idiots! What have they turned us into? Into animals! No, worse than that. For them an animal – even the Toff's dog – has a greater value than the likes of us. Skorobogatov is right: there's only one way out of here – via the crematorium.'

'But not because we're all fools.'

'Alright, so now we're all smart, but what were we thinking before? And now we can see the pie but we can't take a bite! Right?'

'I hate to admit it, but yes.'

'Is there really no way out? Are we doomed?'

'There are thousands of us . . .'

'These butchers have thought of everything. Do you really think it's because clothes are scarce that we haven't got any? They are dehumanizing us. Not only do they isolate us from other blocks, but even from other rooms!'

'That's right, they're afraid of us!'

'Today, at roll-call, one of the interpreters said Moscow had been taken by the Germans.'

'When?'

'Five days ago . . .'

'That means Moscow is holding out. It's a hoax. They want to break our spirits completely. How many times have we heard "Moskva kaput", while actually they're talking all sorts of rubbish.'

Vanya Zimin – a restless and resilient fair-haired guy about twenty years of age – returned from the latrine, slamming the door: 'The bastards! They're fishing everything out of the food canisters again!'

'Then you go tell them only rascally scoundrels act like that!' came a voice from one of the bunk beds.

'I'm not doing that!' Zimin replied, 'I never have any luck anyway. So far I haven't once got either grain or meat.'

'Of course not, they fish it all out.'

'That's all right, there'll still be beetroot in it. They're fools and don't understand that there's a lot of cholesterol in meat but beet-root contains vitamins . . .'

Fishing out what was most edible and nourishing from the food canisters was a daily ritual performed by the interpreters. They would do this in a leisurely fashion, right in front of the inmates the food was meant for. And the soup wouldn't be distributed to the rooms until this ignoble procedure was completed. Everyone did his best to stay in his room so as not to see this disgusting operation. Only unbearable necessity would drive some to the latrine, but they'd make the trip at a run, there and back, so as not to catch sight of the open canisters, which released an aroma that made mouths water and empty stomachs contract in cramps and spasms.

Zimin was a live wire. The most optimistic gang in the room would gather around him. These guys found the strength to joke and laugh: in doing so they cheered each other up. They occupied all their spare time with conversation and reminiscences, doing their best to distract themselves from gloomy thoughts. But the soul of the party was Alexandrovich, an inexhaustible storyteller, with his bosom buddy 'Chavoito' – so-called because he always used the expression 'Chavoi-to?' ['Whassat?' – trans.] when he failed to catch what was being said. There was also Kolya

Govorov, seemingly from Belorussia, and Viktor Kouznetsov from Rostov, among others. People crowded round this core as if at a cosy fireplace.

The bond between Alexandrovich and Chavoito was strong. They were from the same area, were equally educated, and had become POWs under similar circumstances. Furthermore, both men had a beautiful wife and a pretty daughter. But as for the rest, that was a different matter. Alexandrovich had lost his parents in early childhood. He'd travelled widely, seeing and experiencing many things. Chavoito was the only son of his parents and till recent times had lived with them, having never ventured far from the town he'd been born in. But he was well read and mature. Even in the current situation Chavoito kept his humour and was a real joker. With his big, sensitive, responsive heart, Chavoito was always ready to help others, and consequently enjoyed the respect of his comrades. But people didn't just respect Chavoito, they loved him too. Indeed, it was impossible not to love him for his open heart, compassion, and his ability to understand how a comrade was feeling: for with just a word he could touch a man's innermost feelings. Indeed, Chavoito could delve into the depths of an exhausted soul and draw out something precious: hope. In this way he kept alive confidence in the final victory of our Motherland, which he loved strongly and passionately.

Chavoito was also loved for his songs. Alexandrovich once jokingly declared that Nature had her true sons and her stepsons. She'll give one person a kind heart and good looks, a musical ear and voice, and many other positive features; but then she'll give another one thing only and nothing else. Chavoito had been lucky. He was not just Mother Nature's true son, but a favourite son. And he sang remarkably well and soulfully. His voice could capture not just your ears but also your emotions. Chavoito's songs brought both joy and sadness. Listeners would laugh and weep. At these moments he was directing the mood of the company like a conductor his orchestra. Chavoito especially liked to sing, *If Her Friend Is Wounded the Girlfriend Will Avenge Him in Combat*. He always sang softly, and most men would whisper along too. Chavoito had another special gift. He was a natural born actor and his mimicry was astounding.

Alexandrovich was respected no less than his friend. But in contrast to Chavoito he was serious and silent. He was a listener, and only rarely offered an opinion, which was always taken into consideration. However, Alexandrovich would change completely when, by request, he began telling stories or giving speeches. Then he could talk for hours, and the others would listen with bated breath, forgetting about everything.

But some contrast in personalities didn't inhibit the friendship of Alexandrovich and Chavoito. Really, they seemed to complement one another. Physically, Alexandrovich was fitter. But Chavoito would make the room smile by staging real performances with Vas'ka 'Golovokrut' [Head-turner – trans.], nicknamed for his rare ability to do various head movements while keeping time with any tune (in August 1942 he would, as one of a small group, make his escape from Birkenau).

After some time spent in silent reflection, Chavoito announced: 'I wish I had a medical education.' Mocking him, Zimin asked him to repeat, piping up with, 'Chavoi-to?', meaning, 'Whassat?'

'You heard, you Siberian chipmunk.'

'Do you know what a chipmunk is?'

'Of course I do – it's a bear.'

'You're a bear yourself! Alexandrovich, you tell him what a chipmunk is, because he doesn't know the difference between a fir tree and a pine tree and is trying to put on the mantle of Jules Verne.'

'Is it true that Jules Verne never set foot outside his home town?'

'It's true – but he wrote about the whole world.'

'Chipmunks are a small agile animal similar to a squirrel. They're very scared of heights. If one is in danger and jumps up a tree, he rushes about on the branches giving out a piercing whistle.'

'There you go, exactly right, Van'ka!'

'So why do you wish you were a doctor?'

'I wouldn't be lying around now but increasing my knowledge.

What opportunities there are here for the study of the human body! It's a museum of anatomy with unique specimens. Look at this, for example . . .' Chavoito, wearing a serious frown, turned to Alexandrovich, 'A suitable research subject. He is of undeniable interest.' Poking his friend's chest with a bony forefinger, Chavoito continued: 'In here, in this cage, behind the natural protective grill whose bars, if I'm not mistaken, are called ribs, a fine comradely heart languishes in captivity. Based on my scant knowledge in this area I can competently state only one thing: the subject has quite a thick skin, and as you will kindly see for yourselves, a hairy covering of uncertain colour despite its thickness. There's nothing surprising about that. It's a basic and characteristic sign of atavism. Man originates from the monkey, from the animal, that is, from cattle. Thus, this variety of livestock's descendant . . .' Alexandrovich slowly raised himself up on his elbows, clenching his fists, and Chavoito – stopping mid-sentence – prudently retreated: 'My apologies, my tongue ran away with me!' Alexandrovich shook his fist in front of Chavoito's face: 'Just watch it!' Chavoito's eyes followed his friend's fist with an astonished expression: 'Look! Look! He's got a fist as good as the Toff's, only it's black for some reason . . .'

'Who can say why a woman cries for joy, cries for grief, and cries for resentment too?'

'She can't get by without it, brother,' Chavoito broke in again, 'they've got a well developed organ that produces water like a machine, for tears in unlimited amounts.'

'Well, that's not right. I've known one you couldn't squeeze a teardrop out of!'

'Everyone cries. Maybe they don't do it openly, but deep in their hearts they do for sure.'

'And where do the tears made by that organ pour to?' someone asked cunningly.

'Where to? Hmm, where to . . . This organ certainly has a complicated layout and it directs tears somewhere past the eyes and into the stomach.' Everyone burst out laughing, the creator of the complicated organ theory loudest of all.

'Chavoito, tell us something a bit more cheerful.'
'D'you want to hear my friend's humorous story about wives?'
'Of course we do!'
'Here we go. A humorous story by Alexandrovich entitled, *You Be the Judge*.' And with Chavoito's introduction, Alexandrovich began:

I've got my own opinion about wives. It has developed as a result of my personal experience and observations. I tried to find confirmation in books, but I guess this issue has been muddled up in them quite deliberately. But you can't fool me! I'll always draw the line between white and black! It's shameful they're praised as tender creatures. It's shameful and ridiculous. Does it mean that my wife is a tender creature as well? Hee-hee! Very funny! Maybe someone has a tender creature as his wife, but not me or my neighbour. Van'ka – beg your pardon, Ivan Ivanovich – my neighbour from the same apartment, once said it would be more correct to call a panther a 'pussycat' or an owl a 'dove' than to call our wives 'tender' creatures. And if he, Van'ka, had the right, he would prohibit books about wives on principle. And rightly so! Many of them, I'll tell you straight, are unworthy of the time and energy spent on them. Sure, in olden days, tsars and nobles used to run the show, and wives enjoyed no equality or liberties. If they were written about, it was all out of pity. But what about now? They don't deserve it! May I drop dead if they deserve it! They abuse this equality. They even try to climb up here, as far as our necks. And God help us if they finally jump on top of us – it would be easier for a horse to throw his rider than a husband his domineering wife! You are smiling? You don't believe it? You wait, the time will come and you'll find out.

And now I'll prove my case with some facts. I've got a friend called Sasha. Maybe you've heard of him – Sasha 'Koudryavi' ['Curly-haired' – trans.]? Lots of people know him – he's a good guy. But once an evil spirit inspired him to get married out of the blue, completely unexpectedly. He came to my place like a man who already had experience of family life, all smug and smirking: 'I'm getting married today!' Well, my wife wasn't at home, so I gasped loudly. In vain I tried to talk him out of it: 'Think it over, don't ruin your young life. Look – the sky is overcast today and a crow is croaking over there – no good will come of it!' But he just laughed and said: 'I am a modern man and am not superstitious. And it's not friendly to put spokes in the wheels of my fortune. You'd better give me your blessing as a friend.' I replied from the heart: 'I haven't got an icon to bless you with but I've got a candlestick – a really heavy one – to knock some sense into you!' Guess what? He got offended! He didn't even offer me his hand! Off the sucker went to get married.

One evening I chanced to come across him in the street – he was running and glancing back. I called to him with due decorum: 'Good evening, Alexander Petrovich!' – 'Ah, it's you, hello!' He looked pale, unattractive, his suit was crumpled, hair tousled, his eyes burning and his hands trembling. I said: 'What's wrong, Sasha, it looks like you've been stealing hens!' – 'You can laugh if you like but I wanna cry.' – 'From happiness?' I asked with spite. 'I was a fool not to listen to you,' he said, 'for that crow was croaking for a reason – it was prophetic. My life's been wasted in the full bloom of my years. You, my friend, may smack me on this ugly, hateful mug, for I can't look at it any longer.' – 'What happened? Did she turn out to be a man?' – 'Worse than that! Oh! It's a shame to tell you about it. It appears I wash my face wrong and there's last year's dirt in my ears. And I don't brush my teeth right, so my mouth stinks like a cess pit – nasty to kiss – and my feet smell of sweat. And my fingernails? She said you could grow turnips under them! Well, I could put up with it, if it was just at home. But we went out for a walk. Of course we walked arm in arm, sedately – as I thought – and with dignity. Suddenly she pulled her arm out from under mine: "Are you a husband or a muff?" she hissed. "Husband," said I, tingling all over from her ferocious, cutting look. "Now that you're a husband, don't stare at young girls. They are so-and-soes and only know how to snatch away husbands from decent wives. I'm not a dunder-head – I see all that – and won't let my husband get led astray." On we walked, me looking mostly at the ground, for I'm afraid to look around. Then she stops and goes for me again: "Don't walk like a bear at a country fair, and don't wave your arms like a soldier! Keep your head up, because that's not just anyone next to you, but your wife! Be proud and glad of it. I'll make a decent man out of you! Let's go – I'll be watching your every step!" I was so embarrassed I don't remember how we got back home. And there I got the riot act again. I don't remember how I managed to escape! Now I'm gonna relax . . .'

A month later I came across him again. Sadly there was no chance to talk to him. I was riding a tram and he was walking down the street. I wanted to jump off but they wouldn't let me: 'Comrade, there's no stop here!' they said. Time passed and I encountered him again. Now he looked fresher and neater. Chest out, and with a more cheerful look. Surely he was having another break from the nightmare of family life?

Poor fellow! Like me, he'd gotten used to his wife as an inescapable necessity. Really, you be the judge! So what if my feet stink? It stinks even worse in some lavatories – pardon the expression – and we put up with all that. Or consider the teeth. Brush them every day? Try to polish them with a brush every day and you'll probably spoil them! And how will you get by without teeth? They're too petty, those wives, too petty! They're unworthy of the ink and good paper wasted on them. May I drop dead! Unworthy! They make fun of the likes of us and that's a fact! So, you could sooner call an owl a 'dove' . . .

As soon as Alexandrovich finished his story, a listener picked up the theme: 'There are some wives like that. For real! I knew one in Samarina Balka, in Mariupol. And she was worse than a tigress.

Her husband would come home tipsy and she'd be at him: "Where have you been? Who have you found to get you drunk?" And so on, and so on. She'd jump on the poor man and bash and yell with all her might . . .' Suddenly someone cut in: 'Guys, the Student's dying!' Everyone scrambled down from their bunks.

The 'Student' – as we called him – was one of the group of optimists. Earlier that day, after morning roll-call, he'd been beaten by an SS-Mann for giving a black look while the brute chased some cripple with a stick. He was beaten unconscious and had been lying like a corpse ever since, his limbs twitching every now and then in nervous spasms. But his brain was still working, engaged in an inner struggle, as betrayed by the tiny movements of his open mouth. But now the lips were blue, and understanding his struggles were futile, the boy was staring at those gathered round. His clear eyes, wide open, expressed pain, anguish, supplication, and an awareness that this was the end.

It's hard to endure an ordeal like that. Everyone was silent, hiding his thoughts and emotions. Pity, sympathy, condolences, were pointless. Again the body shook with convulsions. The intelligence in the eyes faded, dragging the lids half shut. Someone tried to close them but they opened again in a final act of defiance. Then came the last gulp for air. A moment later and the eyes grew dim . . .

'Fare thee well, friend! Only this morning you were remembering your university friends, joking and cheering others up. It's an ignoble hand that cut short your young life. We'll remember all this and we won't forget. Fare thee well, friend.'

'And no one will know where your grave is . . .' Souslov shot to his feet: 'So we're gonna snivel are we? Or maybe we should beat our heads against the wall? That's just what these vermin want. We have to hold onto life with our hands, feet, teeth, and spirit to spite them!'

'Quiet! The Toff's coming . . .'

Once, during evening Appell, we discovered that the Toff was going to celebrate his birthday. We were told about it by a guy from another room who'd been sought out by an interpreter as a professional butcher. 'Have you ever killed a bull?' the Interpreter asked him in the Toff's room. 'I have,' replied the former butcher, 'no trouble at all.' – 'And what about a ram?' – 'Of course! Why, it's the easiest thing in the world! They're silly animals . . .' – 'How about a dog?' The man was taken aback: 'Why would a butcher kill a dog? If it's old it'll die on its own. If it's young but useless the best thing would be to finish it off with a gun . . .' Suddenly his gaze fell on a small dog perched on a chair, calmly watching everyone with clever eyes. 'We're all going to roll-call now,' said the Interpreter, 'you'll stay here. Don't go near the windows. You'll put the skin, head and legs into that bucket. You'll cover it all with this piece of paper. You'll do the dressing and cutting in the latrine. Wash away the blood so as not to leave any trace.'

Next day a loud voice made us prick up our ears. Our room was opposite the one occupied by the Interpreter and the Blockältester, so we always heard when someone was visiting them, and tried to foresee the course of events from the tone of their voices. We could hear a lot of laughter, which didn't bode well, especially as we could hear Blockführer Baretzki – the White Hare – laughing loudest of all. Suddenly the door to our room swung open – the orderly barely had chance to jump out of the way – and the White Hare barged in, accompanied by the Toff and another man. Behind them a gang of interpreters gathered in the corridor.

The White Hare was smiling through thin, tightly clenched lips. His eyes were cold and unseeing, his ears were red – his eyelids even redder. The stink of strong alcohol filled the room. The orderly screamed 'Achtung!' and everyone froze. The White Hare's staring eyes began sliding over faces and bodies. I was lying on the third level of bunks, next to Souslov, and when the monster's gaze fixed on us my heart sank. I suddenly felt hot, dizzy. Blood pounded in my temples. A thought flashed through my mind: 'Is this really it? Is this the end?' A strange weakness gripped my body . . .

'Raus! Raus!' ['Out! Out!' – trans.] I came to my senses with a start. The White Hare was no longer standing next to me but slowly swaggering away down the aisle, poking his finger at something and hissing 'Raus!' Gently touching my arm, Souslov whispered, 'Better go, buddy . . .' I don't remember climbing down from the bunk, or walking into the corridor, but Souslov was behind me. A few others followed one at a time. An interpreter lined us up against the wall in order of height. Souslov was first in line, I was second. The White Hare and his cronies quit the room and the door closed, cutting the last visual connection with our comrades who'd remained behind. I didn't hear what the executioners standing opposite were saying – if, indeed, they were saying anything. As if entranced, I was staring at the Toff's hands: slowly, slowly, he was putting on his gloves. A thought pierced me: 'Here it comes, the end.' My legs were so weak they barely supported me.

Smiling obsequiously – and with a theatrical sweep of his right hand – the White Hare bowed to his colleague, as if to say, 'Please, begin!' At that moment I recognized the very same officer who met us on the first day, the one who'd killed our comrade. His name was Hans Stark, a Gestapo officer, and his presence was the reason Baretzki was trying so hard.

Stark squared up to Souslov. Keeping his hands behind his back, Stark slowly rocked from heel to toe. Suddenly Souslov gave a sharp grunt and keeled over, writhing in pain: Stark had kicked him between the legs with a steel-toed jackboot. A step to the right and Stark was swaying in front of me. This was the first time I'd seen him close up. His lips were tightly clenched and the small knots of muscles in his cheeks throbbed convulsively. Savage hatred smouldered in his narrowed eyes. I wanted to spit in his face. And this desire soon welled into an overwhelming urge to strike, to make the brute suffer at least an atom of the pain his victims endured. My heart was drumming, and my degraded dignity was shouting: 'Hit him! Make him understand that he is dealing with a human being!' But my mind protested: my blow would not reach the target; he would prevent it; and that would mean certain death, as well as the execution of my comrades. The price would be too high. But were these thoughts prompted by reason or cowardice? No, not cowardice – I'm not weeping with fear am I? I'm not begging for mercy: even though death is staring at me through Stark's squinting, bestial eyes. Suddenly something flashed before my face, followed by a shower of sparks, then pink and red circles, then darkness . . .

Stark's fist had punched me between the eyes, on the bridge of my nose. I'd lost consciousness immediately, the force of the blow smacking my skull into the wall behind. I regained consciousness a few moments later. Barely managing to open my eyes – gummy with congealing blood – I saw Souslov squirming on the floor nearby and immediately recalled everything. A thought burned through me: 'Don't move, don't show any sign of life. Only patience can save you.' Fortunately for me, when I came to my senses the punishment was already over. Remaining face down, and squinting through my right eye, I saw the White Hare approach Souslov and put a boot on the man's throat. Souslov found the strength to raise his hands, grasp the boot, and throw it off his neck. The Toff kicked him between the legs and someone else kicked him in the head. Laughing like lunatics, the butchers returned to the Toff's room. One of the interpreters opened the door of the orderly room: 'All of them into the mortuary! Quick!' I don't know what they did to the others but only three of us were left alive.

Once, after a sleepless but nightmarish night, I dozed off on a lower bunk in the middle of the day. I slept so soundly I didn't hear the orderly's 'Achtung!' nor the Toff entering the room. One of the guys lifted his arm to nudge me. Too late – the Toff noticed his movement, threatened him with his fist, then strode up to my bunk. Even the hush that descended on the room failed to rouse me and I slept on, lying on my side with my mouth open, facing the aisle where the Toff stood with a cigarette and lighter in his hands. He stared at me silently, then, smiling, he opened the lighter and pulled out a piece of cotton wool soaked in petrol. He was about to pop it into my open mouth, when, at that moment, I grunted, ran my tongue around my teeth, closed my mouth, and carried on sleeping. The Toff carefully put the cotton wool on my naked side and set it alight. I jumped up with pain and fright. I jumped so hard my head struck the planks of the upper bunk, lifting them, and nearly tearing through a mattress made of paper wadding. According to my comrades, when the Toff saw the expression on my face he split his sides. Delighted with his joke, he left.

Another time I was room-orderly. The orderly's duty was to yell 'Achtung!' when a Blockältester or Blockführer came in to inspect the room or the cleanliness of the windows. It was around 11am. I'd been desperate to go to the latrine for a long time but was hanging on because the Toff's whistling warned me he was pacing back and forth along the corridor. A 'window man' stood by each window, constantly wiping the already spotless window panes. Despite a chill wind, we were supposed to keep the windows open all day, in order to circulate clean air. The 'window men' were responsible for wiping the glass and shutting the windows when it was safe to do so. I stood at the door, keeping my ears open for the Toff's whistling and pacing, and giving signals by which the 'window men' would shut the windows when his footsteps grew fainter and open them when they grew louder.

The whistling was coming nearer and nearer. The windows were open, the 'window men' wetting the glass with saliva and buffing them with paper. As usual the Toff opened the door with a kick. I immediately yelled: 'Achtung!' The Toff silently looked the room over without entering and went away whistling. I shut the door and the whistling died away. I signalled the 'window men' and the windows were shut tight against the freezing wind. I was just about to run to the latrine when the door suddenly swung open – the Toff stood on the doorstep: 'Aha! I knew it!' he pronounced triumphantly. He then turned to me: 'You're the orderly? Lie down here.' It all happened so unexpectedly, I hadn't even had time to give the 'Achtung!' The 'window men' rushed to the windows, swinging them open, but it was already too late. The Toff must have guessed our game earlier and crept up without whistling, taking us unawares. Now I was standing in silence and inwardly burning up. I couldn't take my eyes off the Blockältester's kid gloves . . .

I lay on a table, on my belly. The Toff took a 2-metre stick – used for carrying the soup drum – and selected a convenient spot for a hit. It would have been possible to kill a bull with such a stick, given enough room to swing, but fortunately the low ceiling hampered the operation: but even so, such a beating might prove fatal given my weakened constitution. My mind swam, feverishly seeking a way out. What to do, what to try? My heart clenched after the first clout on my buttocks. My body became limp, my knees bent, it was difficult to breathe. Resting my head on folded arms I saw the Toff's pink face: his blue eyes twinkled with pleasure and his thin lips looped into a grin. There was no point expecting mercy from this sadist with the girlish complexion. The heartbeats pounded, sending blood thumping to my temples, and I was covered in a cold sweat. I saw the Toff raise the stick for a second strike. What if he hits me on the spine? I'd seen people suffer and die from such a blow. He knew it too. Maybe he'd try it right there? My thoughts raced: 'What to do . . . what to do?' The acute pain in my overfull bladder, compressed by the weight of my limp body, gave me a life-saving idea: I should immediately simulate loss of consciousness. And so I moaned, shut my eyes, and after a minor effort sensed warm liquid under my body. An instant later urine began trickling off the table. Noticing the piss spilling from the table and splashing on the floor the Toff lowered the stick. Grimacing with disgust he shoved me off the table with his right foot: 'You Russian swine!' Then he spat, removed his gloves, and quit.

Affording the sadists amusement like this was, in psychological terms, nothing compared to their favourite torment, which usually involved everyone in the room. Whereas the former treatment, more often than not, ended with the deaths of those to whom it was meted out, the latter rarely ended with an immediate fatality. This torture would begin on a command from an interpreter: 'The whole room – outside and line up!' No respite, no deliverance: in a few minutes everyone – including the sick – would be standing along the corridor wall, eyes fixed on the door of the Toff's room, nerves stretched to the limit . . .

Is it really going to happen again? Everyone is trying to guess, but just as a drowning man catches at a straw, we catch at a thought: 'Maybe they've lined us up to announce something?' Our tormentors know that time is also torture. They keep us waiting. Silence. Not only does silence reign in the corridor, it also commands in all the adjacent rooms, where prisoners remain frozen, straining to catch any sound: perhaps they will be lucky today . . . ?

The door slams. The premonition has proved true: the White Hare and the Toff stand before us, carrying long whips. A cold spasm ripples down my spine. An agonizing moan shatters the silence, followed by hysterical weeping – a man's nerves have failed. The butchers are not touched by that. They crack their whips in the air, making gunshot noises. The interpreters rush to line everyone up with their backs flat against the wall – slaps, punches, abusive yells. At last everything's ready. Smiling, the Toff steps aside in deference to the White Hare. The torture will commence. The line of dirty-grey bodies is frozen, arms stretched down and palms pressed to the wall – that's the order. Our heads are thrown back, eyes closed: it's easier this way. Waiting for the blow is the most terrible thing, the most tormenting aspect of corporal punishment. Waiting for the blow is a test of your will power, a trial of your nerves. Any failure means death.

The prisoners stand in silence. Below protruding ribs and sunken bellies the White Hare's gaze falls on the little bunches of our genitals. Today these are the centre of the sadists' attention – the bull's-eye these beasts will be doing their best to hit. To score a hit on such a target requires skill when wielding a long whip. Even practised sadists rarely achieve the desired aim. Most lashes end with a loud crack, having failed to make contact. A few catch the belly or pelvis. But one or two hit home, releasing a spasm of wild delight in the executioners. Any strike slices open the body. A smack on the scrotum is the most painful. And everyone in the line expects such a strike, while hoping for a miss. Fortunately for the tormented, the sadists observe a rule: one swing each. It saves many but lends cruelty and fervour to the flogging. I'm number seventeen. I flinch with every crack of the whip, counting them up: one, two, three, four, five . . . A burst of laughter and unintelligible babble. I open my eyes and, rolling them without turning my head, see the White Hare give way to the Toff. That means they've agreed to swap after every five attempts. I'll be flogged by the Toff. A sharp moan through clenched teeth muffles the Toff's triumphant exclamation: 'Sehr gut!' Now he is yelling: 'Drei!' A shot. 'Vier!' A shot. 'Fünf!' 'Oh!' And another muffled groan . . .

The corridor was filling up with moans, sobs, and hysterical weeping, which wouldn't subside even for the shouts of the butchers. I was lucky – the whip cracked without touching my body. When the sadists are passing by, you must stand still. The first time they subjected us to this torture one of my comrades lost consciousness and fell on me. Instinctively – not having time to consider the consequences – I caught him, losing my balance and falling on my extended arms. At the same instant I heard a crack next to my left ear and felt acute pain. I shot upright straight away, noticing blood dripping on my shoulder: the whip had cut my ear open like a knife. And yet I was happy: it could have hit me on the eye.

For over a week I remained deaf in that ear, but that was nothing compared to a terrible misfortune that befell a comrade. Physically fit and sturdy, this man had been a sailor. He was blinded by a blow on the head from a stick. We brought him back to the room unconscious, and after washing his blood-stained scalp, left him dozing quietly. In the morning he couldn't see a thing, though otherwise he appeared quite normal. At first we didn't believe him. The irrepressible Chavoito remarked: 'He's probably as blind as the Wise Hare.' – 'What Wise Hare?' someone asked. We turned towards Chavoito: 'The one who told the Bear about his ailment. Haven't heard it? Really? Then listen up':

The Hare is running through the forest, full of joy, cutting capers and jumping with glee. The Bear is slouching towards him, nearly weeping with sadness. 'What's the matter, Mikhalych?' says the Hare, 'what disaster has befallen you?' – 'You shut up, Squint! ['Mikhalych' and 'Squint' are typical nicknames for the Bear and Hare in Russian fairy tales – trans.] I was drafted an hour ago.' – 'Too bad,' replied the Hare, 'I was rejected as unfit.' – 'How come?' – 'I can't see, so I'm completely exempt!' – 'What d'you mean "can't see"?' – 'Very simple! Look, there's a tree over there, all dried out on top. Can you see it?' – 'Yes . . .' – 'Well, I can't! Not me!' And the Hare, skipping away from the astonished Bear, disappeared into the bushes . . .

Many of us laughed heartily at this unpretentious story, but the bitter reality soon depressed the common mood again. It was painful to see our blind comrade – who couldn't himself believe he'd lost his sight – stumbling about the room, banging into bunks and people. And whenever he bumped into someone, the sailor would snatch hold of him and ask if it was day or night, and why it was he couldn't see anything? It was horrible to see the eyes in his tormented face – normal-looking but lacking vision. Running out to evening roll-call we seized the sailor by the arms. The Blockführer and Blockältester stood in the corridor, driving people with shouts and blows. In the commotion the sailor got left behind on the stairs. The last comrades to come up dragged him outside, already dead.

Days passed. The crematorium, smoking night and day, couldn't cope with the growing workload, and the stench of death penetrated our room through the open windows. After the roll-calls dead bodies were no longer taken away as before, but dragged down into the basement to await their turn to be burned. Once or twice a week they'd count these corpses, moving them to the other side of the basement. I had to take part in this death-tally.

Usually about ten of us worked in the cold, damp basement, under the supervision of the Blockführer and the Blockältester. We worked like an assembly line. Two men prepared corpses for moving, two stacked them into piles, the rest shifted them two by two. The counting had to be done quickly, but we were hampered by rats. Big and ferocious, they had no fear of men: only sticks and whips would send them scurrying to hide among the corpses or into dark corners. Even so, some rats put up a fight and our work would stop. Then the Blockältester and his buddies would boldly attack the rat, which would retreat with an angry shriek, evoking triumphant exclamations from the pursuers, who rushed into battle with great zeal every time.

The work in the basement took a heavy toll – and not just physically. Trapped in a well-thought-out system of constant violence, daily harassment, and outrages against human dignity, in an atmosphere of unpunished murder, where death was always at hand, we became immune to its horrors. This may be hard to believe – and seems implausible – but it confirms that habit really is a monster. But we had never wondered what became of the dead or murdered after their demise – there was no reason to think about it. That was why our encounter with the corpses of our comrades, with whom we'd just been sharing all the ordeals befalling us, caused such a painful reaction. And it was all the more poignant because most of them had died a violent death, a fact strikingly obvious from the injuries visible on their naked bodies. The traces left by the rats looked horrible too. It was impossible to look at them without a shudder. Meanwhile a thought – importunate and fearsome – gnawed away at us, causing heartache, inhibiting breathing, constraining muscles and fogging consciousness. It was impossible to get rid of it, for each corpse suggested the same thing: such a fate awaits me too. But when? It was hard to contend with. It demanded an enormous effort of our weakened wills not to lose self-control. A wild, spiteful hatred, born in the jungle of the camp and buried in the depths of my tormented soul, burned my body like fire.

One day, in the second half of November, a rumour flew around the camp: everyone was to undergo a check by the Gestapo. One of the blocks was already being done. Since there was no communication with our comrades from other blocks – even the ones situated nearby – any rumour or information was conveyed through the grapevine during roll-calls. We struck lucky: during an Appell our block was lined up next to the one that had already undergone the procedure, so our comrades gave us all the details concerning the interrogation. At the evening roll-call this news was forwarded down the line.

Thus, when our room was called up – along with the others in the block – and we were hurried, naked, through the camp in a column, we knew we were being taken to the Gestapo. This was our first foray outside the area where roll-calls were conducted. Here we saw two-storey buildings made of red brick with windows wide open. Everywhere was neat and clean, the gravel footpaths separated from neighbouring lawns by thin wire. No one was around, apart from a few lonely, miserable-looking inmates in dirty striped outfits. They were walking slowly, scrutinizing the ground. We realized they were cleaners – even a matchstick would be picked up and taken away.

We found ourselves in a large, light, ante-room. Despite the open window we felt like we were in a sauna. We hadn't experienced such bliss in a long time, and although plagued by painful uncertainty, were glad of this moment of quiet, and of the warmth caressing our bodies. Most of us had already learned from bitter experience a skill familiar to veteran athletes: to use any opportunity to relax the muscles, switch off the nerves, and fall into reverie, while remaining alert and ready for any surprises.

There was an interpreter with us, half-Polish, half-German, all scoundrel. He was constantly doffing his cap and clicking his heels, greeting each SS soldier who passed through the door to the Gestapo office beyond. We knew they'd begin interrogating us any minute. We also knew we had to answer all questions quickly: any hesitation, any suspicion, and we'd end up in a punishment bunker somewhere. Petr, who'd been taken on by Oberkapo Bruno during the very first days for coaching in English, was one of the first to land in that bunker. But no one knew why. One of our comrades, who knew a bit of German, was the first to tell us of its existence. He'd been interrogated with another comrade but at different desks. After he'd been dismissed, and was already leaving the room, he'd heard an SS officer at the other desk yelling furiously: 'This is a Kommissar, a Communist! Into the bunker with him! The bunker!' We'd heard the bunker was for torture, and afterwards, the firing squad . . .

The first two disappeared through the door. Every two or three minutes an SS orderly would let the next person in. Our interpreter set up a queue before the door. I wormed myself forward, right up against the door, so as to shorten the agonizing suspense. Suddenly the door opened and I received a shove that sent me staggering forward. The reflector of a table lamp dazzled me. Two men sat at a desk in shadow. One was writing something. The second officer, with a cross under his chin, stared at me. The death's head on his collar gave off a dull sheen. A voice barked: 'Surname, name, patronymic, year of birth, place of birth, places of work, occupation, which year joined the Communist Party, education, where graduated from military school, knowledge of German . . .' Although I knew the questions in advance, and had prepared answers to them, the force of this verbal torrent nearly knocked me over. The questions were asked in Russian, and someone behind my back kept yelling, 'Quickly, quickly!' The officer observed me, occasionally whispering to his neighbour – the one who wrote without lifting his head. The voice continued: 'Tall stature, black hair. Special marks? Aha, here we are! Above the back of the left palm there's a tattoo – 1912. Is it your year of birth? Give me your right hand. Turn around, you!' The Interpreter was behind me. He vigorously poked my fingers into black ink and made fingerprints on a piece of paper. 'Off through that door! Next one!'

Sighing with relief I went out, and in the next room heard the following: 'Stand over here, up against the wall.' There was a table in the middle of the room. No SS men. Several inmates in clean striped outfits with green triangles on their chests were branding those who'd been checked. 'Surname? Correct. Now you are number 1418. You can forget your surname but remember the number.' Two men came up. One of them pressed a small block against my chest, above the left nipple. On this block was the number 1418. The digits were made of short needles with the blunt ends fixed on plates. When the first man pulled the block off my chest, the second rubbed black ink into the holes left by the sharp needles. I emerged into a corridor where I encountered my comrades, who'd also come out with the same black spots on their chests.

That evening the empty bunks in our room were filled with guys from another block, who'd undergone the same check. A list of numbers, rather than surnames, was made for the Blockältester. It was the first 'nominal' count over that whole time. After several days, when everyone had been through the Gestapo interrogation, we learned some shocking news: according to the branding only about 9,000 Russians were left . . .

At the end of November we were rushed off to a bath-house for the first time. It really had been a bath-house but there was no hot water – only cold in both the taps and the showers. Bathing became yet another humiliation: stripped naked, despite the bitter cold, we were herded to the bath-house by our captors. When we refused to wash in the freezing water they turned the fire hoses on us, blasting us with icy jets from high pressure nozzles. Aiming at our eyes, ears, mouths, and bellies, the cold water cut, choked, burned and blinded. Those caught by the blasts writhed and fell, seeking salvation under benches and behind the bodies of those who'd dropped unconscious.

After this ordeal – bodies blue and eyes red, feet and hands numb with cold – we were marshalled into a room like so many cripples. There they shoved into our hands military blouses, pants and boots. At first I thought it was a hallucination. I couldn't believe it and my comrades were going through the same thing. A booted kick in the small of my back made me throw my hands around the whole bundle and run on around a corner. The room was filled with an unusual buzz. The dirty blouses and pants, all faded with sweat, breathed out something near and dear. After all, this stuff was ours – Soviet from the very fibres to the stars on the buttons. Someone stood with his back to me. His shoulders, sharp from the bones sticking out, suddenly shuddered. He wept aloud, kissed the blouse, and wiped his tears with it. And he was not alone. A few minutes later and we couldn't recognize each other. For two months we'd been absolutely naked, and got so used to seeing each other without clothes that now it was difficult to recognize each other. Here we chose foot wraps and field caps from a pile – the luckiest ones even got puttees.

We returned from the bath-house excited and cheerful, paying no attention to those among us who shivered uncontrollably, eyes wide, bright and glassy. Only later, back in the room, did we understand that clothes would not save us from the consequences of our cold water treatment. Almost a third of the room fell ill. The sound of coughing, moaning, and delirious shouts filled the room. Some poor guys jumped from their bunks and tried to run away. It fell to us, the fittest, to organize watches night and day, in order to protect those frenzied with fever. Similar things were happening in other rooms – all had been subjected to the icy bathing – and there was no doubt this suffering had been inflicted on us deliberately.

At this very time we often heard shooting at night. Dozens of people, mad from sickness and in delirium, were killed for stepping too close to the prohibited area by the fence. Others died on the electrified barbed wire or simply froze to death, wandering deliriously around the camp. The percentage of sick unable to walk was so high that, for the Russians, roll-calls now took place indoors. The Blockführer, escorted by the Blockältester, would do the counting in the rooms. To make the task easier, everyone lay down across a bunk with his head to the aisle, up to five men on each bunk, in three tiers. On the lowest tier the dead and the sick, regardless of their condition, were laid the same way.

Meanwhile, mortality from abuse committed for amusement stopped, but mortality from the cold increased. And lice appeared in our clothes. Their numbers grew with irresistible speed. We'd kill them for hours but with no result. To this day I can't recall it without a shudder – you'd give your blouse a sharp jerk on the collar and feel them pour down your belly. We were scratching our bodies raw. And then the most terrible thing arrived: typhus. We didn't even notice the start of this epidemic. Later we worked it out: death had come disguised in a form dear to our hearts, pleasing to our eyes – soaked with Russian sweat and blood, it had arrived with our clothes. Now typhus was raging and people were dying in dozens. The sick and the healthy bedded down beside those who'd succumbed to typhus. Our captors weren't interested in how many were fit or sick. We dragged the corpses down to the basement ourselves, where hundreds of others were already awaiting cremation. Auschwitz's only crematorium smoked around the clock.

One day, Viktor Kouznetsov – we slept next to each other, sometimes in each other's arms for warmth – ran back from the latrine, agitated as never before. His eyes gleamed with some invisible fire and his face beamed a broad smile: 'You know what I've discovered?' he said in a furtive whisper. 'What's happened?' – 'It's amazing!' – 'Well, tell me now!' Viktor rubbed his hands with glee, smirking darkly. Suddenly his expression changed and he spitefully threatened someone with his fist. Alarmed, I looked around, asking: 'Are you in your right mind?' – 'Of course, what a question!' Then he continued: 'You know, if it were in my power, I'd pin a medal on the clever fellow that put out this idea. Just think! We can infect these SS vermin with typhus lice!' Immediately I grasped Viktor's proposal, and his mood. It was a surprisingly simple idea and within our means. Our lice could be used as a weapon. And what a weapon! Thank you, Soviet man, my countryman, my brother in arms, blood and misfortune. Thank you for this good idea, as heartening and encouraging as a breath of fresh air. For the first time in two months we had a real chance to avenge the deaths of our comrades, to avenge our sufferings. We rejoiced like children at the thought of retribution.

We immediately discussed the details and logistics of flicking typhus lice at our tormentors. Several others were also briefed, and we conducted a 'firing exercise' with lice. The results surpassed all expectations. The best way of flicking or 'firing' the lice was with the middle finger off the thumb – the finger movement was barely noticeable. And the best position was from a lower bunk, the range being quite sufficient. We contemplated all possible ways the administration might do checks: the Blockführer and Blockältester might walk along the aisle and count together, or the Blockführer might do it alone while the Blockältester stood at the door, or the other way around. We prepared ourselves for two days and then started 'shelling'. At any favourable opportunity we fired at the SS men, the Toff, and the interpreters. The lice were kept in a paper bag.

Very soon the results showed. First, the interpreters began to fall ill. When the White Hare fell ill we nearly danced for joy! This success buoyed us up, but dulled our caution. Everyone around talked of nothing else, and people began flicking lice in all the other rooms: it was impossible to restrict this spontaneous manifestation of revenge. Deep down, everyone thought that he was firing the most infectious louse at the hated enemy; that just by wishing it, one or another butcher would fall ill and pass to the next world.

But our triumph was short-lived. Some base coward squealed. We were convinced of this when new measures were introduced for roll-call. One day the interpreters opened the door and announced from the threshold that the routine for counting would change from that day. At a given signal, everyone would have to lie down on the bunks as before – facing the aisle – but now they'd have to put their chins up on the side planks of the bunks, holding them with both hands, fingers spread wide. Anyone who failed to cooperate, or who moved his fingers, would be punished with death. Now the interpreters, armed with whips, would keep a close watch on us while the Blockführer counted. The slightest movement resulted in a savage beating, frequently resulting in the death of those who'd fallen under suspicion . . .

Meanwhile, typhus still ran wild. The blocks occupied by Russians – where the epidemic raged like fire and death wandered the rooms unchecked – became a place of terror, not only for the gaolers but also the prisoners, who'd seemingly experienced the worst. The sombre fame of these blocks was confirmed by round-the-clock visits from carts, unable to carry away corpses fast enough. Our buildings were fenced off from the rest by barbed wire and avoided by all. Soon there was a shortage of voluntary interpreters: so Poles were forced into our zone under threat of retribution.

At the end of December the death of some SS men, or fear of the epidemic, forced the camp administration to open a special hospital for Russians in one of the blocks. From the windows of our room we watched the exodus of sick stagger over for treatment. Of course, everyone hoped for help, for a cure.

Soon our room became empty too. Not only the sick, but also those suspected of being infected, had been taken away. The rest were issued paper and stinking paste to tape up the chinks in the windows. A rumour spread they were going to fumigate. Next day they ordered us to get undressed, hang all our clothes on the bunks, and be ready for the bath-house. We ran to the bath-house in trench coats and boots on our bare feet. But our bodies were so stiff from the biting wind that after a few moments we could hardly budge. Our feet moved only by sheer will power. But we recovered in the bath-house. The water was barely warm, but at least the previous humiliation wasn't repeated. And we were allowed to wash for two or three hours while the block was fumigated. Everyone was very glad. There were no SS men nearby and the servicing inmates kept a respectful distance and didn't come close. Our trench coats were disinfected in a neighbouring room.

And so we returned in a cheerful mood. But all night we suffered from the fumigation vapours lingering in the room. Neither open windows nor draughts helped. We gulped fresh air at the windows for as long as the severe cold would allow. Then we ducked back into the warmth, giving way to others, before returning to the windows again. Our heads ached and we began vomiting. That terrible night seemed to last forever. We weren't allowed to turn on the light, there was unimaginable crowding in the aisles, and it was like that till morning. By sunrise nearly a third of the room's number lay motionless with blue lips and blackened faces. Most of them died without coming to their senses. It was the same in the other rooms.

CHAPTER FIVE

Birkenau

One dark morning, several days after the night of horror, we received a sudden command to get dressed and line up outside. At first we thought it must be an outdoor roll-call, but this was disproved by the second command: the sick, when dressed, were to line up in the corridor. We already knew from bitter experience that separating the sick from the fit was never done without a purpose. As for the hospital set up for Russians, no one ever came back, supporting the rumour that patients were not treated there but killed off. Now everyone feared the hospital. Consequently a ripple of unease spread among the sick when the order came to line up in the corridor. The rest of us – those who were still fit – got dressed and went outside.

Although it was January, the weather was comparatively warm and windless. Fine snow was falling, covering the ground with a fluffy white carpet. All of a sudden, angry shouts in Russian, Polish, and German erupted. The sound of heavy blows echoed around us. Our captors had decided the Russian lines were not arranged smartly enough, and laying into men with sticks and fists, had caused a stampede. But eventually the columns formed up and the Blockführer began his count.

By the time daylight broke, we'd been standing for more than an hour, our muscles growing stiff from lack of movement. Suddenly we heard the command: 'Right face! Quick march!' and moved off in rows of five. They marched us out of the zone occupied exclusively by the Russians. Once again we saw the beautifully ornate iron gates ahead of us. Three months ago we'd entered this hell through them. What else did Fate have in store for us? Maybe we'd be sent to another camp? At this thought my spirits revived . . .

Like children we walk hand in hand, so as to preserve our rows of five. The head of the column has already passed through the gates. We follow. Nazi Officers count the passing heads from both sides of the column. Beyond the gates soldiers with rifles, wrapped up in warm winter uniforms, form up to escort us down a long, empty street. In a daze we stare at the houses with their window curtains. It looks warm and cosy behind those curtains. Did we really used to live like that? When was it? It seems many years have gone by since then. The shrill whistle of a steam train. We cross several railway lines packed with trains, into an open field covered with snow. The dirt road is rutted. Brown puddles and lumps of dirty wet snow are everywhere. We avoid them with difficulty, for any break in formation is met with fierce abuse by the soldiers. We advance over the field towards a small thicket. Mounds of quarry stone, bricks, and road metal are strewn over a huge area. Ditches and trenches filled with water cut the field this way and that. Prisoners in filthy striped suits – some in groups, others alone – hack at the hard earth with shovels, picks, and crowbars. Poorly dressed, clogs on bare feet, they look like convicts. Their faces are grey from cold and hunger, their gait unsteady, comical even. And lying in the snow, in the mud, are those whose posture confirms their sufferings have come to an end. It is a horrible spectacle . . .

It turned out we were expected. As soon as the column halted, a large group of physically fit prisoners approached, yellow armbands on their left sleeves. A middle-aged man with a hooked nose, wearing jackboots and a black military-style suit, commanded them in a ringing voice. He also had an armband, on which there was an inscription: 'Oberkapo'. A white square with a number one in the middle caught the eye, as did the green triangle on the left breast of his tunic. Here, too, it was an inmate surnamed Bruno who had the first number in the whole camp. Brutal, merciless, sadistic, he enjoyed the full confidence of the Camp Commandant, and as we later discovered, controlled the fates of all prisoners in the construction area entrusted to him.

Our column was divided into several groups. Mine was led by a prisoner with an armband announcing him as a 'Vorarbeiter' – that is, a foreman – to one of the ditches where those who'd arrived before us worked silently, paying us no attention. Thus the Soviet POWs began their first day of work on the construction of a subsidiary to the Auschwitz camp, known as 'Auschwitz II' or Birkenau, although the Poles called it Brzezinka.

The area was flat, waterlogged, and covered with moss. To the west was a dense but stunted copse, behind which flowed the Vistula river. Some 3–4 kilometres to the east ran a railway line, with some city beyond. To the north and south there was the same flat area. Only recently the Polish village of Brzezinka had stood here: now no trace remained.

Relishing the change of location, as well as the relative freedom, we began digging a trench to drain the water. We worked along-side the old hands. Emaciated – just like us – and with the same drawn, sallow, faces, the expression in their eyes betrayed a single emotion: despair. How could they stand, move, work? What strength supported them? This first encounter aroused our suspicion: these were dead men working next to us. Maybe we didn't look much better, but living so close to our comrades on a daily basis we'd grown accustomed to appearances. We hadn't noticed what was so clear on meeting these fellow-sufferers: death was clinging to our shadows.

At first it seemed the old hands paid us no attention, each man minding his own business. But several times I sensed that someone was looking at me. Eventually I swung round and met the eyes of a tall, hunchbacked prisoner, digging a few metres away. I knew he wanted to say something, and was only waiting for the right moment. When our Vorarbeiter went off for a smoke, the hunchback came closer, pretending to look for something with which to clean his shovel. Suddenly he whispered in broken Russian: 'You mustn't work like that, tovarishch [comrade – trans.], you mustn't! Save your strength. Watch this . . .' When he was sure I was observing him, the hunchback stuck his shovel into the liquid mud, lowered the handle like a lever, and pulled it out again. A few grammes of earth, obstinately clinging to the end of the shovel, were then lifted and dumped on a mound of sticky mud. I looked at the pile I'd shifted and immediately felt ashamed. Within the space of thirty minutes I'd moved more earth than the hunchback and his buddies put together. And indeed, to what end?

During lunch break, when my 800-gramme soup ration had been gobbled up, I established full contact with my neighbour. No one disturbed us – the Vorarbeiters, or 'foremen', were hanging around the fires where the SS men sat in state. My new acquaintance proved useful: his information helped us understand our new situation. And although the news was not just bad but positively dreadful, it would help us very much in the future.

With the help of our new friends we were made aware of the deadly threat posed by the Vorarbeiters. Mostly louts and scoundrels, whose crooked characters had been revealed in their relations with fellow prisoners, they'd quickly risen above the masses by winning the trust of the camp administration. Knowledge of German had played not a minor role in their promotion, as had slavish obedience to their Nazi masters. Armed with sticks and whips, the Vorarbeiters spent most of the day among us. Essentially our fate was in their hands. They could easily beat someone to death and get away with it by blaming the 'deviant' behaviour of their victim. Indeed, exhibitions of excessive zeal were only likely to win them more trust and encouragement from the SS. Fortunately for the prisoners, not all the Vorarbeiters were murderous villains. A few were decent guys who just made a lot of noise for form's sake, swearing at us in front of the SS men or influential Kapos, and rarely bringing whips and sticks into play. Nevertheless, we were always obliged to observe one strict rule: under no circumstances could anyone simply sit or stand while at work. One might be doing nothing productive, but one had to keep moving at all times.

The day passed comparatively quickly despite the cold, the mud, and the imperative to keep toiling. And at least the threats from the Kapo, the Vorarbeiters, and the SS men were more obvious over here, so some precautionary measures could be undertaken. And there was another big advantage about this new place: the opportunity to communicate with prisoners gathered from all the countries of Europe. In effect, we'd been dropped into a pool of priceless information.

It was already after dark when we returned from Birkenau. Our three months of idleness in captivity had taken its toll, and we trudged back at a snail's pace, leading our exhausted comrades by the arms and carrying those who'd collapsed unconscious. We were also burdened with the bodies of those who'd died as a result of their exertions or been murdered. We were dog tired and barely conscious, so the blows and yells of our escorts had little effect. We moved mechanically, like robots. When they told us to stop, we stopped; when they told us to march, we marched. Blows from Kapo Bruno's stick only made things worse, increasing the number of people we had to lead or carry: eventually, convinced of the futility of their efforts, the Kapos and SS men ceased tormenting us. Eventually our ragged column reached the gates of Auschwitz and was admitted.

In the morning it was straight back to work. Those who failed to get up, remaining behind in the block, simply disappeared somewhere. In the evening they were not around any more. No one wondered where they'd gone – it was too much effort. But instinct warned us not to stay behind . . .

Gradually we got accustomed to the work at Brzezinka. We learned to work with minimal expenditure of energy. We learned how to evade the worst weapons of torture – the stick, the fist, the jackboot – from the mistakes of our comrades, from their blood and deaths. These weapons were employed without restraint. We were beaten by the SS, the Kapos, the Vorarbeiters. We were beaten for bad work, for a moment's rest from fatigue, for helping a fallen comrade, for glaring at our tormenters, and merely for being within reach. To beat the weak and defenceless was considered a sign of respect for the camp administration.

One January day, after the usual reveille, we got dressed and ran outside. The weather was appalling – a ferocious wind was knocking people over. Gusts of icy snowflakes struck our faces as we bunched together on the spot where the column always lined up. There, shivering, we resisted the raging elements with every last atom of strength, while whirlwinds howled between the blocks, whipping up snow in every direction, reducing visibility to almost nil; and the cold snaked its way into the very folds of our clothes, biting bodies with sharp fangs and poisoning minds with foreboding: 'Is it really all up with me?'

My wits grew dull, my thoughts getting all mixed up as we jumbled together trying to find our places, seeking salvation side by side. The thought of a room – a corner – where we could escape these snowy squalls shone like a dream. 'This is the way people freeze to death,' I told myself, 'at first it's cold and painful, then it gets easier until some sensation of warmth appears . . .' The thought there might be an end to suffering subdued my mind, relaxed my body. Meanwhile my heart tapped out: 'The end, the end, the end . . .' But then, piercing the bitter blasts, a voice was heard, choked with glee: 'Inside! Inside fast!' The wind whisked the words away, but the shuffling mass of misery took up the cry: voices tinged with joy, pain, anger, malice all mingled and rushed towards the blocks like an avalanche. Many a comrade failed to return that morning: but a crueller ordeal awaited us in the afternoon . . .

This was one of the worst days of our captivity. We hadn't yet managed to warm ourselves, or come to our senses, when a command was conveyed from room to room to strip naked and form a queue. What was this? The drunken sadists having fun again? Not likely – they wouldn't have warned all the rooms. 'Could it be a fitness check?' someone suggested. An agony of silent waiting set in, a fever of anticipation, for we dreaded a terrible and deadly ordeal. Someone's nerves failed. We heard sobs and a hacking, congested cough. My heart was so heavy I could hardly breathe. Suddenly Zimin broke the silence, angrily letting off a string of foul oaths: 'Fucking bastards! I'd rather have frozen to death this morning!' – 'You can see the crematorium's not working.' – 'The basements have been empty for ages . . .' Disjointed words, reaching us from the corridor, dispelled all doubts: it was a fitness check.

The term 'fitness check' had a sinister meaning in the camp: it signified separation of the weaker prisoners for extermination. It was a regular procedure, designed to rid the camp of souls so reduced they no longer served a useful purpose. We'd already been through this sorting process once before – horrifying in its cynicism – and now we had to endure it again, passing before the butchers on whom our fates depended. That very night they would decide which of us would live and which would die . . .

A fat, middle-aged SS officer sits in a corner of the room by a small table, an enormous peaked cap on his knees. Sheets of paper are stacked before him, apparently containing columns of figures. He looks bored. A clerk dressed in prison clothes – clean and neatly pressed – occupies the seat beside him. Meanwhile, in front of the table, the Blockältester and an interpreter stand to attention, watching the SS man's face with doggish devotion. One window is wide open. Every now and then a gust of wind blows snowflakes into the room, which immediately melt on the floor, darkening into dew. And yet the room is muggy with sweat, as the naked bodies file through the door from the corridor, edging along the walls towards the table. The threshold of the room is our frontier. My turn to cross soon comes. But even before I enter the room my body breaks into a cold sweat: I can see that the fitness check is being supervised by SS-Oberführer Josef Klehr, a medical attendant in the camp – formerly a butcher by trade. Klehr killed my comrade in cold blood for taking a turnip from a passing wheelbarrow, injecting him with a lethal dose of phenol before an 'audience' of prisoners specially gathered for the occasion: 'So perish all who steal!' he announced when the vile execution was over . . .

Quietly yawning in a casual, matter-of-fact way, Klehr passed verdict on yet another man's fate. Brooking no discussion, he usually dismissed his victims with an abrupt nod of the head or wave of the hand. On reaching Klehr's table each prisoner announced his number, then the Interpreter would bark: 'Squat! Stand up! Turn around!' These exercises were very difficult for enfeebled bodies, reduced by maltreatment and malnutrition. It was especially difficult to stand upright after a squat – most were unable to accomplish it unaided and many actually toppled over. And of course, the nervous strain told too. After all, everyone wanted to stay alive, even in the terrible environment of the camp. Meanwhile, the fact that the procedure was conducted in front of dozens of other prisoners only served to heighten the humiliation. The whole affair was a carefully calculated demonstration of psychological ascendancy, designed to intimidate and instil respect for the Aryan race.

At those moments when one faces death, the mind frequently turns to the past. Thoughts and memories crowd in: 'Oh, how short my life has been; how little have I done; what a sad and pitiful way to leave the world – foolishly, pointlessly, and in the prime of life; and all at the whim of this prejudiced, dull-witted, pygmy, who – by the will of a spiteful fate – has been appointed to decide the lives of decent men, many of whom are his intellectual superior! And no one will know what I endured in this hell . . .'

How slowly time ticks by! How poignant it is to take a step, every two or three minutes, towards the fateful spot. It is impossible to depict with words the emotional experience of that moment. The closer you get, the more chaotic your thoughts become, the harder it is to breathe. Your face burns, while cold sweat covers your body. Your heart beats feverishly, hopelessly trying to pump blood through a body numb to sensation. A persistent desire taps away: to kill, to strangle, to tear into pieces this self-satisfied, well-fed butcher, pompously presiding over a pantomime as though it required some special skill. It wouldn't be too hard to kill him. And given the chance, most men standing in the queue would have done it gladly. But no one raised a finger. And not because of cowardice. Bitter experience had taught us the foolhardy nature of such heroics, for it amounted to a betrayal of one's comrades. And so it was camaraderie, heightened by the unbearable living conditions in the camp, which prevented one from doing anything to endanger the lives of friends. It was not a justification of faintheartedness, but a law accepted by all in order to save lives. We didn't discuss this, or even think about, it was a reflex conditioned by circumstances. I could have waited till Klehr sentenced me to death with a casual wave of his hand, then, with nothing to lose, grabbed him by the throat – no doubt others would have joined me in a surge of wrath and hatred – but common sense argued against it. What would it achieve? Experience provided the answer: the consequences would be unthinkable. For an attempt on the life of this nonentity would result in the brutal torture and murder of hundreds of my comrades. And the SS would be only too glad of an excuse for sadistic slaughter.

At last the terrible ordeal was behind me. Luck had smiled on me this time – but with one corner of its mouth crooked with anguish. After all I'd been through, after all that physical and nervous strain, only the desire to get away as fast as possible gave me strength to move – and even to put on a sprightly air.

Once, in February, as we were being marched to Birkenau, a stockpile of winter food for the camp was observed beside the road. It happened that, in one place, the stack was uncovered on the side facing the road. Maybe beetroot had been fetched from here the night before – the wheel tracks looked fresh – and they forgot to cover up the gap with the straw that lay nearby? Maybe a gap had been left because someone was coming back for more? Whatever the explanation, at the end of the day, as the long line of prisoners filed past this spot, a sudden cry went up: 'Beetroot!' and dozens of starving people immediately threw themselves at the stockpile.

Neither the shouts of the Kapo nor the warning cries of their comrades could stop the spontaneous rush. Those who'd managed to snatch a beetroot tried to escape the swarm and hide in the column. Seeing these fortunate ones, more men broke ranks to try their luck. The escorts, initially taken aback, threatened those of us who'd remained on the road with their rifles, shoving us away from the yelling mob. Suddenly a volley silenced the shouts, moans and curses: the SS guards had opened fire on the mass of bodies rooting about in the stockpile. Staccato commands rang out. Beetroot hunters began darting back towards the column as the SS men took post between the stockpile and the road. Behind them, dead and wounded lay scattered among the beetroots on the blackened snow. Someone cursed the Fascists and their Führer: a single shot sufficed to silence him.

The whole drama was over in a few minutes but left us in deep shock. The march back to camp continued in silence. On reaching the gates our duty officer made his report to the officer of the day, who immediately began running along the column with his whip, beating heads and jabbing faces, swearing in every European patois, while liberally spraying us with saliva.

After this incident we rarely managed to pass the stockpiles without casualties. The guards would have their rifles ready on our approach and a sinister silence would set in. Everyone had the same thought: 'Will anyone dash out to face inevitable death?' But in spite of everything, people still ran towards those beetroots. Maddened by hunger, traumatized by suffering, they ran and died under the bullets of the SS. Indeed, the snap of a rifle's safety catch being removed became a sound embedded in my memory. Whenever I heard that abrupt metallic click my whole body would tense up, every nerve screaming, 'Attention! Danger!' And this very reaction saved my life some time later . . .

Twice a day we walked past the scene of these bloody massacres. Finally, after a month or so, the time came when no one dared step out of line. An SS-Mann jeered: 'What, no takers? Does that mean you're not hungry?'

*   *   *

Of the camp butchers – who justified murder under the pretext of 'maintaining discipline' – Kommandoführer Schlange was especially brutal. He particularly enjoyed shooting people with his pistol, accompanying each accurate shot with an ecstatic exclamation. A beast in human form, Schlange was of medium height, stooping, thickset, with a low forehead and small, deep-set eyes sparkling with spite. A constant scowl completed the image of a psychopathic gorilla. He was feared by all those he commanded – prisoners, camp 'aristocrats', Kapos, Blockältesters, and even the SS guards. Rarely did his appearance among us not lead to murder. Once he sneaked up on a group of prisoners who – taking advantage of the temporary absence of their guards – had crowded round a small fire to warm their benumbed hands. Schlange appeared from nowhere. Even we, who were working a few dozen metres from the group, only noticed the Kommandoführer when he began laying into them with a shovel, slaying several on the spot. Others he finished off as they tried to run away. Nevertheless, one of them managed to evade Schlange's blows and run in our direction. Bellowing out a bellyful of obscenities, Schlange followed the fugitive and – standing right next to us – split the man's head in two. Tossing away the bloody shovel Schlange looked around like a wild beast searching for someone else to kill. Then, panting, he turned around and walked towards the road, wiping his neck, face and hands with a handkerchief. We continued working, trying not to gaze in the direction of the sadist.

At the beginning of March the first signs of spring appeared to gladden the eye, but deep in our hearts we were oppressed by the same burden. The number of Soviet POWs coming out to work was decreasing on a daily basis. Death was always lurking nearby. Day and night it snatched away precious lives – at work, on the march, in the block, in the street – aided by the hands of loyal, experienced executioners.

And at Birkenau, on the swampy ground soaked with tears and blood, single-storey brick barracks were growing. The barrack blocks – with only a few small windows, a dirt floor, and a single small stove in the centre – looked more like warehouses than dwellings. Meanwhile the swamp retreated. Part of it, tamped with earth and crushed stone, formed separated flat areas, divided by narrow drainage ditches filled with water. A bitumen road, stretching towards the centre of the compound, began several hundred metres from the drained pads where the barracks were being built. One could easily see from the layout of the road and barracks that the construction was following a meticulously designed plan for a vast complex.

On 15 March we learned that the hospital for Russian POWs had been liquidated over the previous three days. About 500 sick men had been injected with lethal doses of poison. Several former patients, who'd been working in the hospital, told us how this crime had been organized. First, all patients were confined to their rooms. Then, those still capable of walking unaided were called out of the wards. One by one these guys were led into a separate room and injected with fast acting poison. They were told it was medicine and suspected nothing. After a patient had been injected, his body – still warm – would be carried into another room and the next victim led in. The corpses were transported to the crematorium during the night. In the morning the injections were resumed. Those too sick to walk were injected in the bunks where they lay. There were rumours that a convict doctor – German by nationality – who'd organized and participated in this mass slaughter, lost his mind and had been murdered the same way.

Next morning, 16 March, when we were lined up and carefully counted as usual, a group of unfamiliar prisoners took their places among us. They turned out to be comrades – Soviet officers who'd fallen foul of the Gestapo and who'd been segregated into the bunker as Communists. Branded with two German letters – 'AU' for 'Auschwitz' – their lives had been deemed expendable by the camp administration, which proceeded to treat them like lab rats. For example, various experiments – trials of poisons and the accuracy of weapons – were conducted on them. The fact that a small number had survived was a miracle, a wonder of wonders. They looked in better physical shape than the rest of us, but were pale as corpses. For days and nights they'd been left in cells awaiting execution, shuddering at any sound coming from the corridor.

Meanwhile, as daylight broke, the other work parties were marched off, leaving only us Soviet POWs in place. Several SS men stood nearby, discussing something. The Kapos and Blockältesters were there too. No one doubted there was something afoot. The liquidation of the hospital, the attachment of the men from the bunker, and the delay in departing for work were all somehow related. More SS men approached – the familiar sadists: Baretzki, Klehr, Schlange, Merle and the Gestapo man Stark. Then came the command to quit camp. Prepared for anything – even the most unexpected twist of fate – our column slowly snaked through the gates, where guards counted the outgoing men from both sides.

And yet, to our surprise, this day turned out like any other. Only in the evening did we understand the reason for the morning's delay: from now on we were to live at Birkenau. The news was announced by one of the Kapos, as a crew of electricians hastily erected a temporary barbed-wire fence around the brick barracks. Thus, on 16 March 1942, Brzezinka – or Birkenau or Auschwitz II – commenced its life as a branch of the Central Auschwitz Concentration Camp, soon to become famous all over the world as a Nazi death factory.

The first roll-call. There were only Soviet POWs in the zone, so for the first time in five months and ten days we learned our exact number: 666. That was all that remained of the many thousands transported here on 7 October 1941. And most of us survivors were goners, or 'Muselmänner' [i.e. 'Muslims' – trans.] as the SS men contemptuously called all feeble and emaciated men.

Meanwhile, standing in front of our line was a short, elderly man in a striped outfit. Just another prisoner? We paid him no attention. But after roll-call an SS officer spoke to him, and he immediately began shuffling along the line, closely scrutinizing each man in turn. Every now and then he poked a finger into some guy's chest, shouting in Russian: 'Step out of line!' When the 'Old

Man' – as he was immediately nicknamed – came up to me, I felt his gaze slide over me from tip to toe. Indeed, our eyes met, and although I saw no hatred in his stare, I still felt a tingle down my spine. 'Step out!' he yelled, before transferring his gaze to my neighbour. I stepped out and joined those previously selected.

When the selection was over, some twenty-five men – the fittest specimens – had been separated from the line. We remained silent, hearts pounding, mouths dry, eyes fixed on the Old Man and the SS officer, who were discussing something. At last the Old Man came up: 'You're the "housekeeping" labour crew of this camp. I'm your senior. You'll find out tomorrow what to do. In the morning you all leave the barracks at my order. No more than five minutes to get ready. Is that clear?' A second later the crushing burden of anxiety was lifted: another twist of fate had intervened. And the realization that we wouldn't have to walk 3 kilometres, that we'd have a rest soon, was cheering and heartening.

The roll-call over, we ran to the barracks to look at our new lodgings. There was a single entrance door in the middle of the façade. A central passage bisected the barrack block, a small stove standing in the middle. The remaining space was divided by brick partitions into compartments some 2 metres square. Each compartment had three-tier bunks and was designed to accommodate five men. Straw had been laid on the floors of the two upper storeys, but at ground level it was damp, bare earth. Thus the lower cells were used for stockpiling corpses, also in groups of five, to make it easier for the Blockführers to count during roll-calls.

The buzz in the barracks was like in a beehive. We formed into groups of five under the dim light of a single lantern hanging above the stove and occupied the upper levels. The whispering wouldn't quieten for a long while, until, one by one, men fell into the deep abyss of sleep. Then rambling cries, moans, sobs were heard throughout the night; as well as the hushed words of those trying to roll over in the cramped compartments, for space was so limited this could only be achieved by everyone turning at once.

Next morning, when it was still pitch dark, we were woken by loud cries of 'Kommando! Raus!' The Old Man was scurrying through the compartments, hustling people out: 'Raus! Raus!' We tumbled from our bunks and followed him outside to the gates, where two guards were waiting. Then we walked along a narrow-gauge railway track into the morning gloom, the Old Man in front, the SS guards behind. It was frosty, the sky dotted with bright, blinking stars. A biting wind made us move faster. Then the silhouette of a lorry loomed ahead. We were tasked with unloading 50-litre drums from the back of the lorry onto an open railway truck, which eventually rolled towards the camp.

We were on the move all day long: delivering drums and paper bags of bread from the railway, dispatching foodstuffs to the crews, collecting empty drums, washing them and transporting them back to the railway, loading them on lorries.

On the very first day we dismantled for firewood a brand-new single-storey house, standing alone not far from the camp. It was a shame to tear it down. The light, clean walls and the colourfully tiled hearth and stove emitted such a feeling of warmth and cosiness, one's heart clenched as kinfolk and friends were remembered. When they began demolishing the house I quickly climbed up to the attic. There I found Nikolai Pisarev and Pavel Sten'kin avidly looking over the locality through a gap in the broken tiled roof. Pavlik [diminutive for Pavel – trans.] – almost a boy, with a girlish face – didn't even notice as tears streamed down his cheeks. That's where freedom was! So near and yet so far . . .

The transfer to Birkenau instilled a furtive hope in us. It filled all our thoughts. Whereas before, the chance of escape seemed an impossible dream, the situation had changed since yesterday. That night we couldn't sleep, excited by the opportunity given us to actually think about freedom, not just dream about it. The looks of my comrades, full of yearning and hope, eloquently showed this.

Demolition work continued at the house. Iron nails squealed as they were torn out of timbers, walls groaned and creaked, ceilings collapsed, plasterwork disintegrated into billowing clouds of dust. The swearing and yelling of the Old Man was heard everywhere.

Fidgety, zealous, keen-witted, he poked his nose everywhere, hustling with shouts and fists. Small, stooping, beetle-browed, he made a bad impression, aggravated by his use of heavy words or blows for the slightest fault or mistake. By contrast, the troops of the escort crew were surprisingly calm and phlegmatic. They silently dogged our team in its movements but stood aside when work began, never interfering, and giving the Old Man full freedom of action. We couldn't get over our surprise at these sleek-faced soldiers, who'd somehow managed to join the SS, so different were they were from the others we'd come across.

A couple of days later, Birkenau received 'reinforcements', if you could call them that. In the middle of the day the 'Raus team' – as we dubbed our labour crew – was returning from the demolition site. It was a superb spring day. The sun shone brightly, its life-giving warmth melting the snow, transforming our surroundings. We'd barely managed to cross the sticky field leading to the Auschwitz–Birkenau high road when we saw a mob of prisoners at the limit of exhaustion, dragging themselves towards Birkenau. One look was enough to determine they were patients from the camp hospital. No doubt capable of walking unaided at the start of their trek, the road from Auschwitz had exhausted them, for they were moving under great strain. Indeed, this procession was an appalling spectacle. Even we, who'd endured so much and looked worse than anyone, shuddered at the sight. The apparitions walked in silence, lacking strength to cry or moan. Only the rasp of coughs and the clatter of clogs broke the calm. Meanwhile, the bitumen was stained with bloody footprints and littered with tatty paper bandages black with blood and filth . . .

Here comes an unnaturally upright spectre, an aged spirit with the high forehead of a philosopher. His skull is thrown back, his mouth open, spasmodically gasping. His eyes, unseeing, stare straight ahead. Instinctively, his left hand clutches the sleeve of a soul trailing behind, while his right supports a crippled leg smeared with blood. A noble ghoul, he drags a hideous paper-chain of bandages in his wake. Two others shuffle alongside. The first is exhausted, arms hanging, head dangling, feet flopping like those of a puppet or paralytic. The second, supporting his comrade, keeps his balance with a comical gait and an agonized grimace, straining every nerve so as not to topple over. He knows that if his friend falls he'll never rise again. Behind them, others are dragging comrades along like so many skeletal automatons mimicking human movement. Exposed backs, loins, buttocks, betray their extreme degree of dystrophy. Finally, bringing up the rear of this tragic train, the dead and unconscious are dragged along by the arms . . .

Five SS guards escorted the sick prisoners, submachine-guns slung round their necks. But in their hands they carried whips for herding the flock of invalids, taking care to avoid stepping on the bloody footprints and bandages. No remorse or pity showed on their faces. They didn't consider the evil of their actions. They were simply doing their job – a familiar routine, nothing unusual or out of the ordinary. But we couldn't take our eyes off the passing column. Even the Old Man was struck dumb. Indeed our whole team – including the escorts – stood in silence, frozen by the sight of this macabre procession. For many, many years – even now – when I close my eyes I clearly see this terrible scene, which should have been immortalized on canvas to make it accessible to millions, so that it might forever hold up to shame the instigators and perpetrators of this horrible crime.

Despondent, we scraped the mud off our boots and silently walked towards the camp. The Old Man didn't rush us, for no one wanted to catch up with the column of death. And yet, no matter how we dragged our heels, we eventually overtook it on the roadside. Most of the sick were sitting or laying on the bitumen in the most unnatural poses. But some remained standing, scared they'd be unable to get up again. Several were struggling to lift a truck onto the railway track, but it was too heavy for their uncoordinated efforts. Exhausted, they hardly reacted to the shouts and curses of an SS-Mann and stood in-differently, glad of the chance to lean on the truck. We stopped nearby, involuntarily, hesitatingly, wanting to give them a hand. Suddenly the Old Man uttered a frenzied scream, swearing foully:

'Why are you standing there like fucking dummies? Lift it up!' Astounded, I looked back at him. He was unrecognizable with his pallid face, trembling lips, and convulsively clenched fists. Despite his sadistic character, the Old Man – a Pole by nationality – remained a Slav at heart.

If killing is a crime, then what could you call this barbaric treatment of sick, helpless humans? And remember, these actions were not accidental, not isolated, but deliberate and commonplace. It wasn't just genocide but something inexpressibly worse. A man of common sense who has never seen it, never suffered it, can't truly understand the disgusting vileness of those who, directly or indirectly, took part in this brutal war of extermination. What did those unfortunate victims feel? How can one find words to express their suffering? One cannot – it's impossible.

During the following days in Brzezinka the SS men and their devoted camp dogs – the Kapos, Blockältesters, common bastards and criminals – repeated the blackest days of Auschwitz. In the evenings drunken gangs with batons and whips would break into the barracks. There was no salvation for those who fell into their hands or attracted their attention. They attacked with special ferocity the barracks of the Jews and the sick. Dozens of dead and crippled bodies would be left after their pogroms.

From the first days of its formation, the Raus team had been charged with the task of collecting corpses in the barracks every evening, stripping them, loading them on open trucks, and transporting them to the high road along the narrow-gauge railway. After the night raids most corpses had cleft skulls and broken bones or backs. Many of them had suppurating wounds. Consequently it was both physically and mentally challenging to undress the dead and drag them out of the zone. There were Jews, Poles, Czechs, and Slovaks amongst them. There were also our comrades – Soviet POWs whose numbers were falling every day.

And so 30 March 1942 arrived. That day will live in my memory forever. Even now, after all these years, I continue to be amazed: where did I find the strength to live through it? For on that day I didn't just see death, I also felt its icy breath – like a condemned man about to meet his maker.

The day began as usual with the Old Man's shout: 'Team . . . Raus!' It was early morning and the approaching dawn hardly visible. A cold rain was drizzling, the sky overcast with leaden clouds that seemed to bleed into the earth. The Old Man was the last to run out. As usual, he was in a hurry: 'Line-up! One, two . . . March!' First we breakfasted. Then we installed two corner watch towers. After which, we delivered lunch to the crews. And then we collected, washed, and transported empty drums to the high road. After evening roll-call we began removing corpses. First we cleared the lower cell of the barracks, which was occupied by Jews; then we dragged out the Russians. Finally we cleared out the patients' barracks, but this time there were more bodies than usual . . .

The sadists' most brutal raid on this barracks had occurred the night before. When they'd quit camp, we members of the Raus team – including a Polish journalist who'd managed to hide himself among us – arrived on the scene. The air was rank with sweat, faeces, blood. A kind of droning noise filled the room, composed of murmurs, moans, and wordless cries of anguish. Corpses lay in the aisles between the bunks. At my feet a sick man cried for water, stretching out a bony, trembling hand in supplication. With the help of Dotsenko, who was standing beside me, we lifted him onto a bunk. Then Vasili brought water in an empty jam tin he'd found nearby. The invalid gulped it down, his teeth chattering on the tin. I sprinkled some drops on his forehead, and as he regained consciousness the man began to stammer in Polish: 'Stał, is that you?' – 'No, we're Russians from the Raus team.' – 'And where are . . . ?' – 'They've gone. No SS in the camp.' – 'Jesus Maria! They're worse than beasts! But where is Stał?' The sick man looked around feverishly then suddenly shut his eyes. Blindly pointing at a corpse he burst into tears, his bony body shuddering: 'They've killed him! They've killed Stał! Warsaw used to be proud of him . . .' [Stał is a diminutive form of 'Stanisław' – trans.]

It was late when we finished removing the corpses. Although

ready to drop with fatigue, our strength was maintained by the anticipation of rest and the impending issue of our evening ration. Soon we were back at the barbed-wire gates. One SS-Mann opened the lock, another counted us off as we entered the zone and slowly plodded to the barracks. As luck would have it, I was the first to reach a ditch full of water, which ran parallel to the fence. Day and night we used this ditch for washing, so without a thought I squatted down and dipped my hands into the water. Suddenly, among a number of sounds, I subconsciously caught one that evoked a defensive reflex action. In the fraction of a second occupied by a short metallic click, I received a warning: beware of a bullet. Sensing that it would come from a watch tower, my body instantly recoiled as the shot rang out. At the same moment I saw, rather than felt, my left hand jerk backwards. It all happened in front of my comrades, who, being only a second behind me, were still approaching the ditch. Everyone dashed back into the shadows.

Under the dull light of a torch I examined my bleeding hand. I *couldn't* believe my eyes and *wouldn't* believe in such an absurd event! Was it real? Not a dream or hallucination? There was no physical pain – the emotional hurt suppressed it. I vaguely remember someone walking me to the sick quarters, where patients gave me enough paper bandages to make a dressing. The bandages immediately went blood-red, so they continued wrapping the wound until the wad grew big and heavy.

In six long months of imprisonment this was the first time I'd sensed the approach of death so keenly. It had always been near, but I'd never realized how hard it would be to face. Now this was the end: nothing would save me, nothing would stop the tragic conclusion to this ridiculous event. Meanwhile I felt a leaden heaviness in my hand as the heartbeats pounded in my head. Nightmares began to torment me: Klehr gloating over a syringe, coming up to me smiling; gas emanating from the bloody lump of bandages; an infection spreading, as they wheel me on an open truck towards the crematorium. And all the time, reverberating round my brain, a voice calling: 'The end, the end, the end . . .'

I lay on a bunk in the middle of the barracks, next to the stove. This place was always vacant because everyone knew, for safety's sake, it was better to choose a spot further from the entrance. My comrades tried not to look at me, avoiding my eyes. I understood them well: no one could help and any show of sympathy would only aggravate my suffering. How I envied them! I was eager to live, believing in the defeat of evil and the triumph of justice. I wanted to survive in order to see retribution for all the crimes, suffering, broken lives.

Gradually the buzz of voices died down as, exhausted and worn out, the prisoners fell asleep. But the torment of a restless night awaited me. In such a moment it's unbearable to be alone with your thoughts – they're like annoying flies and it's impossible to drive them away. Whirling with incomprehensible speed, my mind constantly returned to the same matter, which seemed inevitable and imminent . . .

A penetrating stare pierced my troubled mind. Opening my eyes I saw my comrade, Viktor Kouznetsov, standing beside me. I tried to turn over and move my numbed arm. Viktor caught my hand: 'Let me help you . . .' His assistance was much needed, for loss of blood was taking its toll: I was so dizzy that if Viktor hadn't supported me I'd have fallen off the bunk. Then he produced something from his bosom and silently stretched out his hand. There, in his palm, lay three thin roll-up cigarettes. Seeing my joy, Viktor smiled: 'It's from my UR [Untouchable Reserve – trans.]. I was lucky yesterday – I found two cigarette butts.' We both knew how valuable cigarettes were. There could be no better gift in our circumstances: 'Thank you, friend. Thanks . . .' – 'Come on! What a thing to thank me for! Light it up.' Viktor stuck a cigarette in my mouth and ran away for a light. Ten minutes later we parted. I asked him to memorize my family's address, and when he'd learned it by heart, told him what to say to them – if, of course, he survived. Viktor wanted to say something but changed his mind. He looked at me with eyes full of tears, suddenly kissed me, then ran into the darkness. I lit up the second cigarette and drew the smoke deep. My head spun. The keenness of my worries dulled a little. I felt easier and calmer inside. It was as if reality had been shrouded by fog and gloomy thoughts were replaced by reminiscences . . .

The year is 1930. The quiet town of Novocherkassk. Living on a meagre student allowance. There is firm faith in the future, despite the fact we hardly understood the political events occurring around us and constantly argued about them. In a few years I will take my first timid steps in independent work, at a timber processing mill in Serebryanka, near Koushva in the Urals. Later I will be drafted to the 'Special Red Banner Far East Army'.

The boundless steppes and hills of Transbaikalia. After demobilization, the mining sector of No. 3 Experimental Works at Kharkov, producing hard alloys. Scenes and locations replace one another as in a kaleidoscope: Ovrouga, Novoukrainka, Orlova Sloboda; the mine shafts of the Donbass and Moscow provinces; the mercury of Nikitovka, the copper of Degtyarka, the iron ore of Temir-Tau, the tin of Transbaikalia and Kolyma, the gold of Siberia and the Far East. Now the cool roads of the Volga, Don and Amur rivers emerge from my memory; the fascinating beauty of the rocky cliffs of Lake Baikal and the virgin taiga [primeval forest – trans.] of the Amur Province.

And life was in full swing: the construction sites of the first Five-Year Plans were booming. And always I felt like a small cog in a huge machine. But I took pleasure in the knowledge that my work – the work of a former country boy – was useful and necessary. Coming to know the joy of work I was proud that – like an ant – I carried the load that was in my power, participating in the building of a bright and happy edifice, the foundation of which had been laid by the older generation.

And when I was feeling the whole happiness of life, when I'd created a family, when my daughter was born, the war broke out. Dark clouds overcast the skies. Every day brought grief and suffering. The clouds were getting thicker. Everyone lost his peace of mind. How recent it was! My daughter was smiling and waving at me. My wife was crying. Where are they now? Are they still alive? If they only knew what kind of plight I'm in now, and how badly I don't want to die . . .

I couldn't sleep that night. Instead I observed the troubled slumber of my comrades. Their bodies were resting but their minds were still under strain. Not a single sound from outside went unnoticed. Nerves on alert were sensing everything that could bring danger. In the morning, when the usual alarm of 'Team, Raus!' resounded, only those concerned jumped up – most didn't even react. But in the middle of the night it only needed the door to bang from a squall of wind for complete silence to set in: everyone was vigilant for danger – even when unconscious – and only gradually would the sleepers return to the abyss of troubled dreams.

Morning came. Still I felt no pain, but my hand was numb and heavy, as if it belonged to someone else. Fatigue and hopelessness dulled my emotions: the sooner this agonizing suspense ended, the better. Suddenly the Old Man rushed into the barracks. Silently scrutinizing me with a prickly cold gaze he humphed and ran off. He'd probably observed during roll-call that the crew was not up to full strength, and then found out about the SS guard who'd opened fire.

They didn't make me turn out for roll-call. But the Blockführer made sure I was present, as he did for those who were dying, and those who'd passed away during the night. Later, when everyone had gone to work and the block was empty, a messenger came to pick me up. With his help – but with much difficulty – my wounded hand was put in a sling suspended from my neck. I was dizzy with weakness and my legs kept giving way. I trudged behind my comrade as if to the scaffold. Three armed SS men were waiting for me at the exit from the zone, and as soon as I came out they headed towards the high road. I realized they'd just been relieved from watch and had probably been ordered to deliver me to the main camp.

CHAPTER SIX

Hospital

I entered an empty room on the ground floor. Weakened by exhaustion, loss of blood, anxiety, I flopped down on a bench. All was quiet. Before me were two doors leading somewhere, both tightly shut. Suddenly a thought burned into my consciousness: I'm in hospital. Of course! Where else would they put me? Perhaps they'll give me an injection right here on this once-white bench? And then, goodbye life! I heard footsteps. Someone was walking fast. Here comes Death! For the first time I felt a sharp pain in my maimed hand. What should I do? Run away? Where to? Such a display of faintheartedness would change nothing. Was I afraid? Certainly! I wanted to live. But I'm no coward and will do no senseless deed born of fear. Instead I'll just sit. Just sit . . .

Several prisoners arrived, led by an elderly man with a skinny, sulky face. They wore the usual striped prison suits. The old man came up, silently scrutinizing me at point-blank range. Despite an outward appearance of severity, I immediately saw sympathy and compassion in his inflamed eyes. No, this man could not be a murderer, he was incapable of meanness and wouldn't give me a shot of poison. Suddenly I felt a little easier, as if all dangers had passed and a burden beyond my strength had fallen from my shoulders. The elderly man noticed the change. In a firm voice, used to issuing orders and having them obeyed, he asked me in Russian – but with a strong accent – 'Well, Bolshevik, how are things?' Picking up the friendly irony in his voice, and feeling that all was not yet lost, I answered – matching his tone and even trying to smile: 'Couldn't be better.' His hairy eyebrows rose, wrinkling up his forehead. At the same time his jaw dropped slightly and astonishment flashed in his eyes. Suddenly he burst into a fit of loud, contagious laughter. His companions smiled, but the elderly man guffawed frankly and joyfully, wiping his reddened eyes with a handkerchief: 'My colleagues, listen to that – he couldn't be better! That's a Bolshevik for you! Just think, couldn't be better! And that's in his position . . .' Then, cutting the laughter short, he addressed a prisoner in a serious tone: 'Colleague Gurecki, get him on the table immediately. He's got clear signs of . . .' and he pronounced some word in an unintelligible language. Then, turning back to me, the elderly man gave me a wink, followed by a warm smile: 'Everything's gonna be alright, Bolshevik. Since things couldn't be better, we can't let you down!'

The Doctor – and it turned out he was the Chief Doctor of the hospital – went out. The two who remained skilfully and quickly stripped me naked. The left sleeves of my jacket and blouse were cut open, releasing my hand with its pear-shaped lump of bloody dressings as big as a football. Gurecki was especially attentive. A strikingly handsome young man, he was maybe a bit older than I. His clear grey eyes affirmed the sincerity of his words. He spoke Russian well, with hardly any accent, and I would have taken him for a countryman if he hadn't addressed his comrade in Polish. Meanwhile I smiled simply, cordially, openly – like a friend, like a brother.

That was my first meeting with Doctor Alexander Gurecki, a Polish political prisoner who acted as a 'Schreiber' or clerk at the camp hospital in Block 21. Thus Fate brought me into contact with a complete stranger who would become my dearest friend, due to his humane attitude, professional care, and his spiritual, moral, and material support during the most critical moments of my sickness . . .

I walked upstairs to the first floor with the help of Gurecki and

Maria and Andrei Pogozhev, 1940.

In the first year of the war around 3,400,000 Soviet soldiers were captured. According to Christian Streit in *Keine Kameraden: Die Wehrmacht utid die sowjetischen Kriegsgefatigetieiz, 1941-1945* at the end of January 1942 only 1,400,000 survived. The rest were murdered or died from hunger, cold or sickness.

The bodies of the prisoners who didn't survive the journey to the camp were laid out in front of the railway cars.

Barbed wire and electric fences surrounded the camp.

The camp gates with the German sign saying 'Labour Makes You Free'.

A prisoner's uniform.

Reichsführer SS Himmler inspecting the construction of the 'Buna-Werke' plant at Dvory near Auschwitz.

Birkenau prisoners work on the construction of new camp buildings in 1942 or 1943.

Members of the Sonderkommando burning corpses on pyres in pits in 1944.

Birkenau: in this stable intended for 52 horses, 700-1000 prisoners were forced to live.

The 'Wall of Death' between the 10th and 11th blocks where prisoners were executed.

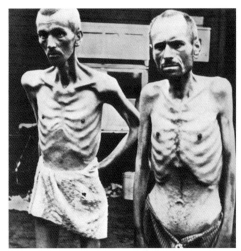

Auschwitz prisoners after liberation by Soviet troops.

Piles of bones and clothes – all that remained of the
1.5 million people exterminated in Auschwitz.

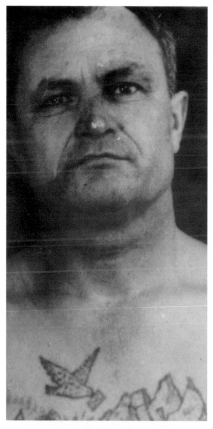

Andrei Pogozhev.

Tattoos on the chest of Andrei Pogozhev, which were made before his escape, to hide his camp number. The scars on his left wrist show where it was broken by a guard's bullet. The dark patch of the tattoo hides the marks showing the year of his birth.

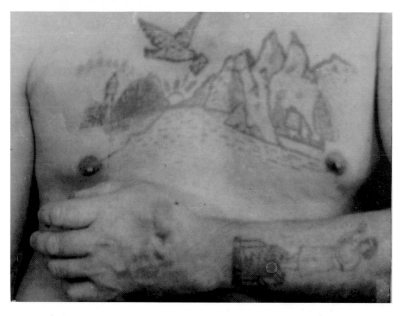

Pavel Sten'kin.

Aerial photo of Auschwitz.

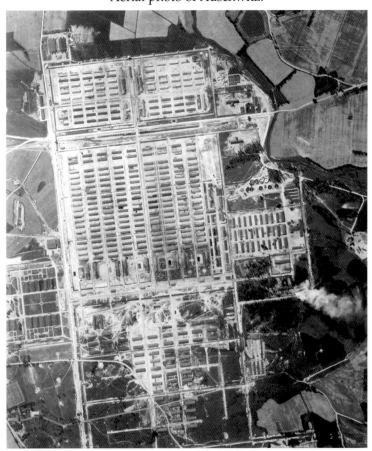

his colleague, entering a large room fitted out with the usual three-tier bunks, from which dozens of sick men stared at me with curiosity. Questions came from all sides. Gurecki – or 'pan' ['Mister' in Polish – trans.] Olek – was readily answering them. But I'd grown so weak from fatigue – not to mention joy at evading death – that nothing made sense: neither questions nor answers were sinking in. Eventually we stopped at a small corner room. Through the open door I saw an operating table, glittering surgical instruments, and the Doctor who'd laughed so infectiously . . .

I'm on the table. They're tying down my arms, legs and body. With great effort I raise my head a little – no SS around, only friendly faces. Gurecki is smiling encouragingly. I try with all my strength not to weep from joy, gratitude, and new-found faith. I try not to, but fail. My emotions break through. But I don't feel ashamed – in fact I'm relieved. After all, they're not doctors but friends, and I have the right to reveal this quite natural human weakness in front of them. 'Hold on, Bolshevik!' I hear the familiar voice as if through a dream, 'hold on, Slav!' I wanted to nod but a pleasant languor had taken possession of me and I just wanted to sleep. To sleep, to sleep . . .

I'm at home with my family. My little daughter is smiling cheerfully, stretching her arms towards me. Two small teeth show white between her pink lips. She's sitting on the very edge of a table and, swaying back and forth, is about to lose her balance and fall. Why am I just watching? My soul is exulting: she is my joy! My beloved one hasn't forgotten me and is stretching her arms so trustingly. And there is so much pure childish joy in her wide-open eyes. Oh! She's falling! I dash forward to catch her. But why can't I reach her? Who's holding me back? Who? My daughter has already understood that she's falling. There is fear in her eyes. She's asking for help. Help! At that moment someone slaps my cheeks. More slaps come – sharply, painfully, jerking my head from side to side. Someone yells: 'He's conscious . . .'

'Where am I? Where's my daughter? Why am I in hospital?' On the floor there's a big basin containing a pile of bloody dressings and lumps of blackened blood. Then I remember – my hand! 'Where's my hand?'

'Here it is, in one piece.' Gurecki lifted my arm and showed me my hand, carefully bandaged with a wire splint. Then he said: 'Thank the Surgeon and remember his name – Doctor Wilhelm Türschmidt.'

'Colleague Gurecki, you exaggerate my merits. We laboured together.'

'I understand, Doctor. But to be sure of saving his life his hand should have been amputated and you didn't do it.'

'Of course there was a risk. But we had to save the hand. Without it, you know he'd perish in the camp straight away. We'll keep an eye on him and undertake all measures to prevent infection. And now what he needs most is rest. Take him to your pentka.' Then, turning to me, Türschmidt said: 'Well, Bolshevik, goodbye!'

'Thank you . . . comrade.'

'Now, now, Bolshevik, don't forget you're in the camp! That word is not to be said aloud here.'

'I said it softly.'

'Well, in that case you'll get away with it this once. Now off to bed.'

I don't remember how they walked me back to the bunks. It was the first time in many months that I fell asleep so easily and light-heartedly. Neither the silence of the night nor the bustle of the day could interrupt my sleep, which lasted about twenty hours. After months of exhausting nervous strain the miracle of falling into caring hands had heralded a complete collapse of my physical and moral strength. Gurecki later told me that he'd tried to wake me; Türschmidt had come too: but he'd said everything was fine, since my pulse and breathing were normal, and that sleep would be the best medication for me.

In the hospital block the main common hall occupied one-half of the partitioned first floor. This space was divided into five segments, each one known as a 'pentka' – the Polish word for

'one-fifth' [more correctly 'piąty' – trans.]. Based on the com-
position of its patients my pentka could be described as
'international' in character. An engineer from a Prague broad-
casting station, Kazemir Stahl, lay next to me on the second tier
of bunks. A Pole – a former newspaper editor – lay across the
aisle. Above him, on the third tier, was a major general in the
Polish Army, who'd been aide-de-camp to the Governor-General
of the Amur Province [in pre-Revolutionary Russia, when Poland
was part of the Tsarist Empire – trans.]. This man had once been
responsible for exterminating tigers in the Ussury area of eastern
Russia, and on his right arm was a tattoo – executed with great
skill – depicting the head of an enraged tiger with open maw. But
as well as this artistic memento, he also bore a different kind of
souvenir from his encounter with the big cats: an obvious limp.
Nevertheless, he was a sturdy, big-boned old man, who climbed
the upper bunk without assistance, despite his declining years.

In front of us, on the lower bunk, was a Jew from Amsterdam, his
jaw broken by a blow from an SS-Mann. Other companions included
two Frenchmen – one of them was called de Chevalier – plus a Czech
soldier and a young Portuguese officer. The latter was a very handsome man, the son of a colonial official and an Indian woman from
Borneo. He arrived the day after me, with no obvious signs of sickness, and in the following disgraceful manner. When Gurecki walked
the Portuguese to his bunk he suddenly broke into a fit of swearing.
Howling indignantly and flinging every oath, the mongrel created a
shameful scene. Kazemir Stahl, who was proficient in several
European languages, including English, interpreted. It turned out
that this scumbag didn't want to lie next to 'filthy Frenchmen' as he
expressed it. Above this insolent fellow were a Jew and a Pole. The
latter was called Skiba or Skaba – a mighty athlete and former
member of the Polish national squad. Two other Poles were above
him. One was a cavalryman, who, as I was later told in secret, used
to occupy a senior position in the regular Polish Army and was an
active anti-Fascist. He was absolutely fit and was hiding in the
hospital under an assumed name.

In that huge hall, containing hundreds of patients, I was the first

Russian from the Soviet Union. Thus, most were seeing a Soviet citizen for the first time. Naturally, many wanted to view me up close, being eager to discover what sort of people the Soviets were, who'd been fighting a bloody war on their native soil not just for their own freedom, but for the freedom of all.

On the very first day pan Olek put me under the care of the Polish Major General, but forbade any long and tiring conversations. The General spoke Russian well and was sociable in the way of old men. He was a great conversationalist with an excellent grasp of international affairs and human nature. Listening to him I found the peace of mind I so desperately needed in my situation. But not only was he a captivating story-teller, he was an attentive and thoughtful listener too. And he knew the pre-Revolutionary Far East better than I. When I told him about Komsomolsk-on-Amur [an industrial city of the Amur province built in the 1930s – trans.] and Khabarovsk, about life in the remote mines, lost in the thickets of the taiga, he compared it with what had been there a quarter of a century ago, being sincerely surprised by the changes that had occurred during Soviet times.

Next day the 'organizer' of our section – so-called because his job was to 'organize' the procurement of everything that was in short supply – managed to carry out an errand for Doctor Türschmidt, obtaining some ampoules of anti-gangrene medicine. They injected me with this stuff straight away, pan Olek thoroughly examining my hand several times a day: 'Andrei, you were born with a shirt on! [Russian equivalent of the English expression, 'to be born with a silver spoon in one's mouth' – trans.] And that's after such soiling of the wound! Oh, our Doctor is a wizard!' – 'Is he a German?' – 'No, he's Polish, body and soul. His name is German but he's from Tarnów. I've been told by one of his colleagues how much he was loved there. When the Gestapo arrested him the whole town wept . . .'

After a day or two the rosy mood in the hospital – facilitated by rest and the feeling that I was out of danger – was destroyed. And so dramatically, the events of that day left a deep scar in my memory, illustrating that the hospital was still part of the same terrible extermination camp. First thing in the morning of that ill-fated day a nervous buzz broke out. A message had come to us via clandestine means, announcing that the Chief SS Doctor would make his rounds later in the day. Such rounds were usually made two or three times a month and their purpose was the same as a camp fitness check: dozens of death sentences passed without trial or investigation.

After giving me another injection of the anti-gangrene serum Gurecki dressed my wound, leaving few bandages, and briefed me on how to behave during the round: 'Most important – be calm. Look straight into his eyes. Convince yourself that it's not a butcher before you but a stranger. And don't hide your hand. On the contrary, put it where it can be seen. It's not very likely, but if he asks something, answer briefly – yes, no, and nothing else. Well, good luck . . .'

Judging from the words of eyewitnesses, the SS Doctor favoured a straightforward procedure. Accompanied by Türschmidt, the ward clerk, and an SS orderly, he silently inspected all the bunks. Türschmidt was required to report the nationality of each patient and his condition, plus the length of time he'd spent in the hospital and his expected period of convalescence. Then, with hardly any questioning, and based on considerations known only to himself, the SS Doctor would either proceed to the next bunk or casually ask the patient's number. This apparently innocent inquiry, which consisted of a single word – 'Number?' – amounted to a death sentence. The doomed man's card would be handed over to the clerk and his camp number daubed on his arm with a chemical pencil. After the SS Doctor's rounds all those selected would be issued their food ration, but everyone knew their hours were numbered. In the evening they'd be called up and led away.

The most fearsome aspect of the whole exercise was the apparent randomness of the selection. It seemed much depended on the SS Doctor's mood and the impression made on him by particular patients. Only this could explain why terminally ill men were frequently ignored, while those who were getting better heard the Russian word for 'number'.

About 10am an oppressive silence descended on the hospital. Clerks and medical orderlies took their places in different parts of the hall. Ordinary doctors waited in the operating room, while Türschmidt nervously paced up and down the wide central passageway. An outstanding therapist and surgeon who'd given his life to the noble cause of saving others, famous far beyond the bounds of Poland, he was suffering on account of this cold-blooded killing of his patients, on whose lives he and his colleagues had sacrificed so much time, energy, experience and ability. Suddenly a stooge shouted through the door: 'He's coming!' Türschmidt straightened his clean prisoner's jacket and stood at the entry.

'Achtung!' Türschmidt quietly submitted his report in German to an officer in SS uniform. The SS butcher, barely listening to Türschmidt, fussily inspected the passageway, the doctors (who were all standing to attention), the floor, the bunks and even the ceiling. Then the round began and everyone froze. There was such silence in the hall that voices were clearly heard from the street outside. Türschmidt was speaking clearly and quietly as usual, following the SS Doctor from one bunk to another. The dull word 'number', breaking the silence like a thunderclap, struck at my heart. Who was the first victim? Within the space of fifteen minutes I counted five condemned. My heart ached from the approaching danger, the blood pounded in my temples and especially in my left hand, where the blood vessels had been torn apart. Time dragged agonizingly slowly. I tried to think about something else – anything – but my mind immediately returned to the horrifying reality. At last my turn came. 'A Russian from Birkenau. Accidentally wounded in the zone. Been in the hospital two days. In good condition . . .'

The SS Doctor looks at me point-blank. He has a clean-shaven, oblong face. From under a snow-white gown silver skulls and lightning bolts glint ominously on his black collar. A high-crowned cap with its small lacquered peak covers his forehead. Cold grey eyes reflect cleverness enslaved – an intellect but no flight of ideas. Just for a second something flashes in his eyes at the word 'Russian'. From his calmness, his lack of visual reaction, it's clear this terrible procedure is customary for him and causes no remorse. Looking at this intelligent face under different circumstances it would be impossible to guess that it belonged to a cold-blooded murderer, merciless and brutal. But one has to find the will-power not to give away one's thoughts, to coolly look into the eyes of the butcher on whose whim one's life depends . . .

The silent torture lasted no longer than thirty seconds. The fiend's glaze slid away and I sighed with relief, having caught an encouraging glance from Gurecki. Now it was my neighbour's turn: 'A Jew. Lower jaw is broken . . .' – 'Number!' The SS officer interrupted Türschmidt and stepped up to the next man. 'A Pole. Acute inflammation of the hip. Condition satisfactory. In the hospi . . .' – 'Number!' The round lasted about an hour. The death sentence was passed on more than thirty patients.

After some time, when the condition of my hand raised no more worries and, as the Polish doctors were saying, it had begun to 'suppurate well' [i.e. produce pus – trans.], I began observing the way of life in the hospital. Despite the visits of the SS doctors – dangerous predators – the hospital was a piece of paradise compared to the outer camp. I found this contrast striking. While in the sheer hell of the camp I hadn't even imagined the existence of a place where one could lie quietly.

The special status awarded to the hospital stimulated cautious behaviour among the patients. For instance, all were keen to preserve the prestige of the doctors and medical orderlies, who, although prisoners like everyone else, at least had some oppor-tunity to save lives. On ordinary days the SS rarely appeared and the terrible regime of the death camp had little impact on the hospital. Sick men were examined, given dressings, operated on – just like any ordinary hospital. Everything was done quietly, without fuss, but with great professional skill. This was mainly due to the efforts of Wilhelm Türschmidt and his closest assistant, Doctor Zheltowski. The small corner room, in which my fate had been decided several days before, would, at different times, be turned into an operating theatre, an outpatients' room, or a dressing-post. The clerks of the temporary rooms, or 'Schreibers' as they were also called – mostly doctors with tertiary medical education – kept precise records and knew what had to be done for the patients of their particular rooms.

Since our floor of Block 21 was considered a 'surgical ward', most patients were admitted for phlegmonic inflammations. A phlegmon is a suppurative inflammation of subcutaneous or inter-muscular tissue: in other words, a deep and ferociously painful abscess. This condition was the scourge of the camp, reaping thousands of prisoners' lives. Of course, in a normal body boils and bruises cause no complications: but in bodies starved of vitamins they may easily turn into abscesses. Thus, a blow of any force would cause a phlegmon in most prisoners. The inflamma-tion exhibited its worst form in the large muscles of the hips and buttocks. There the boil would begin from the bone, peeling muscles off the bone tissue. Of course, a phlegmon might start in other parts of the body as well. For example, one young Pole was admitted for a phlegmon on his penis, following a beating. All the efforts of the doctors to stop its development failed.

Apart from me, there were two or three other prisoners in the ward with bullet wounds. For many men, driven to despair, deliberately entered the forbidden zone by the fence, where they were shot by the SS guards. And yet the Germans were nothing if not methodical – any prisoner who showed even the slightest sign of life after being gunned down was despatched to the hospital without fail. There the Polish doctors conducted the most compli-cated operations to save the wretch's life. And they often succeeded: only for the convalescent to be put to death on a caprice of the Chief SS Doctor.

Another SS terror took the form of an eye-doctor, who, apparently impressed by Türschmidt's skills, had decided to become a surgeon. With pure German precision this Oculist appeared punctually at the same time every week. The operating theatre would be emptied prior to his arrival, so he could choose a patient to practise on. Depending on the complexity of the task he'd set himself, as many as three prisoners would find themselves on the would-be surgeon's table. But instead of quickly recovering, most perished. Those left crippled were carried away after the next fitness check. Türschmidt – who had become the oculist's unwilling accomplice – frequently tried to save these victims, or at least alleviate their sufferings, after the butcher had gone.

Thus the Chief SS Doctor and his comrade the Oculist – two highly educated German medicos – brought fear and dread in their wake. But the days when they left us in peace were quiet and serene by camp standards.

I soon became certain that a clandestine organization existed in Auschwitz, which used the hospital as a shelter for Polish political and military figures. In the guise of patients fit men hid in there, and it frequently happened that sick Poles who'd recovered were not discharged for a long time. I tried not to notice how it was done, but sincerely shared the joy of Gurecki and his comrades when they succeeded in operations of that kind.

Several times, at Gurecki's suggestion, he and I went to the neighbouring hall, where, in dark corners, prisoners would question me about the Soviet Union. These men were strangers to me and Gurecki wouldn't reveal their identities. But as Gurecki – with whom I was especially friendly – wanted to keep these meetings secret, I didn't ask too many questions. Much later I recognized one of them as Józef Cyrankiewicz [a leading Polish Socialist and Resistance leader, Cyrankiewicz was imprisoned in Auschwitz in 1942. He later became premier of the People's Republic of Poland (1947–52/1954–70) and afterwards head of state (1970–72) – trans.].

During these encounters, and from daily socializing with other patients – Poles, Czechs, French, Jews, Germans – I became certain of the sad fact that no one had any clear idea about Soviet Russia or the life and customs of its peoples. Repeated malicious slander by the bourgeois press and radio had left such an impact, much of their 'knowledge' sounded like jokes or complete nonsense. That's why the heroic resistance put up by the Soviet people evoked bewilderment in many – especially as the Fascist armies had conquered Western Europe like a whirlwind. Most couldn't understand how the Russians – wretched people by their standards, who dreamt only of freedom and the help of Western civilization – had suddenly begun to defend their Motherland with astonishing valour and steadfastness. For example, the defence of Sebastopol – rumours of which had leaked into the hospital – amazed all by its selflessness. It was beyond the comprehension of most prisoners, who'd survived the time of the Fascist invasion, taken part in the Resistance to a greater or lesser extent, and knew what fortitude and bravery meant. But the defence of Sebastopol verged on madness. Such a struggle could only be made by people for whom the Motherland was dearer than life itself.

Many of those with whom I had occasion to talk openly, heart-to-heart, passionately desired the defeat of Nazi Germany but had little faith in Russia's ability to hold off the German onslaught. Rumours – and reality – lent some weight to this opinion. But my firm and intuitive belief in the invincibility of the Soviet people, their ability to overcome all setbacks to achieve final victory, affected the other prisoners magically.

Of course, this was not the product of my persuasiveness or eloquence – far from it. It resulted from the psychological situation. A prisoner in the death camp needed faith in liberation no less than air. They wanted to live, to return to their families, to take part in the struggle against the 'brown plague'. They wanted to feel human again. And in order to be liberated from this hell it was necessary to defeat the Hitlerite armies in the East or in the West. But the West was silent while the East was desperately struggling. And I – because of how things were turning out – became the representative of the fighting East. Among these sick and deprived people, from nearly every European country, I represented a different social world: the only country to which the eyes of these condemned convicts could turn with hope and supplication. That was the only reason my confidence in the victory of the Soviet people had such a magical effect. It inspired hope, resurrected faith, strengthened fortitude, gave them the strength to beat their illnesses. Understanding this, I tried to uphold their morale to the best of my ability.

But I was not alone in my convictions. One of the most fanatical adherents to the idea of a Soviet victory was a Czech named Havranek – a former teacher of Russian language and literature in Bratislava. He knew Russian history better than I did and was in love with Russia: 'The very history of Russia confirms my confidence,' he would say, 'the words of the great Russian military leader Alexander Nevsky [a Russian Duke whose forces defeated German knights in a battle on the River Neva in 1240 – trans.]: "He who comes to Russia with a sword will die by a sword" summarizes the lesson. These bloodstained brothers of the "dog-knights" [nickname of the Teutonic crusaders defeated by Alexander Nevsky – trans.] will share the lot of the Swedes, the Polish gentry and Napoleon's grenadiers . . .'

Once Havranek got into a dispute with one of the patients, arguing something in German ardently and excitedly. I couldn't understand what the quarrel was about, but knew by their glances and gestures that it concerned me. Suddenly Havranek turned to me: 'Tell us, are there many like you in Russia?' 'No,' said I, 'but many are better . . .' When Havranek interpreted, unconcealed astonishment showed on the surrounding faces, while Havranek's eyes shone with admiration and triumph. I understood that he'd correctly guessed the hidden meaning of my reply, for he didn't question me further, sparing my pride. Later I was convinced that he'd been right.

All significant events – both in the camp and outside – had an effect upon the hospital. Thus the assassination of Hitler's protégé in Czechoslovakia, Gauleiter Heydrich [killed on 27 May 1942 by Czech Resistance fighters parachuted from Great Britain – trans.] reverberated both in the hospital and in the camp as a wave of brutal terror. Nearly all the Czechs and Slovaks, whatever their condition, were led or carried by their comrades out of the hospital. No one knew where they were taken, but there were no doubts that their fate was sealed. And yet, by some miracle, several men evaded detection, including my neighbour, Kazemir Stahl. This young, handsome Czech – a fine comrade – was a man of great character. The content of his soul was reflected in a cheerful, expressive face, and in large, intelligent eyes. Stahl was unable to lie or dissemble. He was always polite and courteous. He could listen when others talked but could also tell captivating stories. Bedridden by a hip phlegmon he endured his disease with fortitude and was an example to us all. It was a surprise that he hadn't shared the lot of the majority of Czechs, but we were sincerely happy about it.

Once we were disturbed by an unusual event. In the evening two Poles from among the walking patients were discharged from the hospital ahead of time by order of the main office. They were immediately taken away and no one paid any attention. But early next morning we saw a large group of prisoners, several dozen men dressed in civilian clothes and black cassocks, and the Poles discharged the day before were among them. The whole group was cheerfully excited. It was clear from remarks overheard and significant gestures that they would be sent out of the camp. Yes, that was something to be cheerful about! Maybe this was the liberation? Maybe . . .

This 'maybe' agitated the patients and evoked the most improbable and fantastic theories. Eventually the selected men were led away. On the same day the 'whisperphone' – as the prisoners called the camp grapevine – produced the explanation. It turned out that all those led from the camp were priests. By all accounts the Pope had heard rumours that Catholic clergymen were imprisoned in Auschwitz, and in reply to his request, Hitler had transferred them all to Dachau.

The most tragic event happened in May. One day Türschmidt received a green sheet of paper – it was a summons to the political department of the Gestapo. Such a call foretold nothing good. Türschmidt knew that.

News of the summons spread like fire. A tense, uneasy silence fell. All eyes turned to the operating theatre, the doctors' room, furtively following Türschmidt's every step and movement. But Türschmidt was calm as usual and kept working as if nothing had happened. In the middle of the day he made his customary rounds – not alone this time, but accompanied by his assistants and the surgeon Zheltowski. Prior to leaving the hospital Türschmidt bade farewell to his colleagues touchingly and with fortitude. It was obvious his heart was telling him that there would be no return, no meeting his friends and acquaintances again. The doctors saw him down to the exit, the patients following with their eyes. Türschmidt quit the hall with wishes for a speedy return: but left forever. The man loved and respected by everyone, who'd done something good and kind for all, had gone. We felt the loss immediately, as if suddenly orphaned. But a spark of hope for a happy outcome smouldered in our souls. No one wanted to believe Türschmidt had gone forever.

The night had gone. Morning arrived. Orderlies were sweeping floors, dusting, wiping window panes. The Schreibers and the orderlies were walking around questioning the patients. The subdued buzz of dozens of people talking filled the hall. Suddenly, one of the men cleaning windows yelled at the top of his voice: 'They're bringing Türschmidt!' A tumult arose. Many men, breaching standing orders, rushed to the windows. With difficulty the doctors and Schreibers restored relative order, driving people away from windows almost by force. And that occurred despite the fact everyone knew standing by the windows was strictly prohibited.

I found myself among the few who were permitted to remain by the first floor window (as we were looking down, the guards couldn't see us). They were escorting a group of maybe twenty people – Türschmidt walking in the rear. My God! It was a bent old man walking, barely shifting his feet, his crumpled clothes covered in dark stains. With his bare grey head nodding as it turned towards us, he seemed to be saying: 'I know that you can see me, I know, I'm sure . . .' The pathetic figure of the once smart and lively Türschmidt evoked a muffled moan: 'You can see they've beaten him, the bastards!' – 'Of course, they couldn't have reduced him to that condition by mere interrogation.' – 'What for? A man like that . . .' – 'Shut up! Back to your bunks!'

I looked around. Most of the patients, especially the Poles, were crying silently the way men do – some openly, others with their faces buried in pillows. The doctors and orderlies were crying too. It was an excruciating scene: sincere grief, indignation and impotent rage. In a few minutes Türschmidt and the prisoners walking with him disappeared into the side doors of Block 11, the block of death wherein comedies of justice were staged, wherein inmates were tortured, tormented and shot.

Two-storey buildings, the blocks of the main camp were laid out in rows stretching east to west. There were eleven blocks in the first row. In the second row, situated north of the first, in front of Block 10 was Block 21, in which the hospital was situated (as I said before, the hall in which I was hospitalized occupied the southern half of the first floor). The blocks for women and children were situated in the first row, numbers 1 to 10 inclusive, and fenced off from the men's camp. The windows of Block 10, facing the hospital and Block 11, were screened by panels. The windows of the first floor of Block 21, facing Block 10, were painted, except for one window of the operation room, which was situated in the south-western corner of the hall. All this had been done to make it impossible to see from the window of the first floor of Block 21 what was happening in Block 10 – the 'experimental' block – and from there, what was happening in Block 11. The southern sides of Blocks 10 and 11 were connected by a solid brick wall about 8 metres high. The northern walls were also connected by a brick wall with large double gates, blank on the inside and made of metal tracery grillwork on the outside. These walls created an isolated yard between Blocks 10 and 11. By the internal side of the southern wall was a black wall with a sandy area in front of it. Executions were conducted against this wall. Most of the yard, and a side exit from Block 11 into the yard, were easily seen from the only open window of the operating room. Thus we could witness the execution of prisoners by firing squad.

Afterwards the corpses were put in coffin-like crates and transported to the crematorium.

As for Block 11, horrifying rumours circulated about this place. People were not just murdered in its basement, they were interrogated and tortured. In this block the farce of German justice was staged. And yet it was here that those lucky enough to be released from Auschwitz – very few in number – were held while their documents were being drawn up. Thus, in a cruel twist, many unlucky prisoners approached Block 11 hoping for salvation . . .

As soon as Türschmidt had been escorted into Block 11 a continuous watch over the gloomy gaol-within-a-gaol was organized. That day was one of the most difficult of my whole incarceration. Everyone was tortured by the same thought: what else could they do to our Doctor? In the evening Türschmidt was shot at the wall. Thus the life of a marvellous man, a skilful surgeon who'd saved hundreds of prisoners from suffering and death, came to an abrupt end. He'd maintained fortitude in all his patients by kind words, good advice, and an encouraging smile. A radiant memory of him will live in the hearts of all who knew Wilhelm Türschmidt, Polish Prisoner No. 11461.

To top off the events of that tragic day Gurecki collapsed. This person, dear to me, to whom I owed my recovery, fell ill. Pan Olek – as he was lovingly called by the patients – would appear at first call to provide assistance. This charming man had exceptional self-control, never argued with anyone, and remained in the background during group discussions – a good listener who rarely spoke up for himself. Gurecki's illness was not dangerous. His nerves simply failed with the execution of Türschmidt, with whom he'd worked since the first day of his imprisonment. He needed complete rest. To my joy, pan Zheltowski gave me the task of nurse and the guardianship of my friend's peace and quiet. Thus we swapped roles. Proud of the knowledge that I was able to do at least something to express my gratitude, I never left Gurecki's side, even when he was sleeping. In fact, his illness made us even closer. We lay together for hours on his bunk, conversing in whispers, and only the need to observe regulations and sleep would separate us.

And what things I found out over the days of his illness! I was not mistaken in my suppositions regarding clandestine organizations operating in the camp. And perhaps the most active were those that involved the hospitals of Blocks 20, 21 and 28. The special status of the hospital blocks within the camp, the peculiarities of their work and stability of their staff, had created favourable conditions for such activities. During the first months of the camp's existence any kind of organization, no matter how small, had been out of the question. Furthermore, all prisoners were oppressed by the hopelessness of the situation and their impending doom. But as the camp had grown, and the number of prisoners had increased, the need to form more or less permanent crews to service the kitchen, the bath-house, the hospital and so on, became obvious.

One of the first Resistance organizations had been formed in the hospital, which offered the most practical opportunity of assisting sick prisoners and saving many from imminent death. This organization, which consisted mostly of Polish prisoners, could maintain communications with all blocks and crews via incoming and outgoing patients. Communications were also maintained via doctors coming from other branches of the camp for medications. Meanwhile, under the guise of patients requiring treatment, prominent Polish personalities – both political and military – could be hidden in the hospital, thus 'disappearing' for a time. And to some extent, the same system worked for sick Poles in need of rest, or those threatened with execution.

Gurecki did a lot of work in this organization. I often witnessed his meetings with prisoners supposedly coming to visit a sick colleague. After a recommendation from Gurecki these men would converse openly in my presence – a circumstance that gave these meetings an innocent character. Knowing neither Polish nor German I wouldn't even try to divine the essence of these conversations. But from the odd word I understood, or the expression on a face, I could appreciate the seriousness of the discussions and the gravity of decisions taken.

It was in those days of pan Olek's sickness, during visits from his numerous comrades, that I first discovered the Fascists had begun mass extermination – not only of prisoners but also of whole transports of people. Apparently the main extermination effort had shifted to Birkenau. They'd set up a 'bath-house' with pipes and a 'shower' grid and turned it into a gas chamber. People would be sent inside as if for a shower, then locked in and gassed.

In fact, the means of annihilating people en masse had been being refined at Auschwitz since 1941. Once, when the camp commandant, Rudolf Höss, was absent, his deputy, Fritsch, tried the effect of a gas–cyanic hydrogen ('Zyklon-B') on Soviet POWs in the basement of Block 11. This gas was available in the camp and had been used to poison rats. The results surpassed the sadist's highest expectations. Further trials, not only in the basement of Block 11 but also in the morgue of the crematorium, confirmed the reliability of Zyklon-B for the process of mass annihilation. In his autobiography, written before execution in gaol, Rudolf Höss wrote that: 'the application of Zyklon-B came as a relief to me, for I would have to start mass extermination of Jews soon, and before that neither I nor Eichmann [Karl Eichmann (1906–62) – the main Nazi perpetrator for the mass extermination of Jews. In 1960 he was abducted by the Israeli secret service in Argentina and later executed after a trial – trans.] could imagine how this action would proceed. Now we had found the gas as well as the way to use it . . .' Fires cremating corpses after gassings in the 'bath-house' burned day and night at Birkenau. The fires and gas chambers were serviced by 'Sonder-kommandos' ['Special Units' – trans.], specially formed from prisoners held outside the camp. No one knew exactly who they were.

Gurecki was concerned that communications with Birkenau had been cut off. A special hospital had been organized there and information had been coming less and less frequently. Many people had been sent to Birkenau from Auschwitz but almost no one had returned.

Here in the hospital it had become possible to establish – with the assistance of Gurecki and his comrades – that prior to the arrival of the first train of Soviet POWs, despatched on 7 October 1941 (in which I had arrived), a large group of Soviet POWs had been delivered to Auschwitz. There were about 600 of them. On 3 September the first experiment with Zyklon-B was conducted in the basement of Block 11. But the initial dose appeared to be insufficient, for on 4 September many of the gassed were still alive. The SS men gave them an additional dose and on 5 September removal of corpses began. But the dead bodies of the gas victims were not cremated – they were taken somewhere. Obviously it had been the remnants of their uniforms we'd seen at the station on 7 October.

The third month of my stay in the hospital was passing and my wounded hand was healing. Following the doctors' recommendations I kept flexing my fingers, even at night, for despite torn ligaments they had to learn how to grip as well as move. 'They must if you want to live!' Türschmidt had told me prior to his death. Meanwhile, my thoughts constantly returned to my comrades in Birkenau. Judging from the rumours I was hearing, very few of them remained . . .

One evening a skinny, stooping prisoner came up to the bunk I lay on with Kazemir Stahl. I'd never seen him before, but he stared at me with sad, expressive eyes: 'Are you Russian?' he asked, in a voice trembling with curiosity and fear. When I answered in the affirmative the stranger continued: 'How long since you left?'

'I left when the war began.'

'And where were you born?'

'In Rostov Oblast province, by the Don River.'

'I'm from Kuban,' said the newcomer, his eyes blinking back tears until suddenly the pain barrier broke and he wept openly, laying his head on the bunk. I looked with surprise at his bony, shuddering shoulders, his thin swollen-veined hands. Stahl turned to me: 'He's Russian, isn't he?'

'Yes,' I answered, 'but I don't understand why he's crying . . .'

'Because I've met a real countryman for the first time in thirteen years!'

'Were you born in Russia?'

'Yes, in Kuban in 1910.'

'Did you leave with your family?'

'No. In 1929 I fled overseas to look for happiness . . .' The stranger grinned, sighed, then shook his head: 'And I found it!' said he, in grim jest. 'I lived in Turkey, Greece, Canada and South America. Everywhere I felt the same: wretched and barely human. Eventually I turned into something worse than a dog. I endured so much misery over those years until life became unbearable. And then came a firm decision – to return home. My heart even became lighter, for I'd found a goal. I did all possible jobs to save money for the trip. I reached France. Then I began to save money for a train ticket. Suddenly, instead of my native land, I found myself in the camp. You can't imagine how homesick I've become. I'm ready for any punishment if I'm only allowed to live amongst my folk and die amongst them in my native land.'

The more he talked the clearer the soul of a man crippled by misfortunes was seen. Thirteen years of rootlessness and humiliation had killed his will, his interest in life, his belief in his own strength and ability. Driven many a time to complete despair, he'd been ready to commit suicide, but lacked the will power even for that. At last he'd made the most sensible decision: to return to the Motherland. He repeated several times that he was ready for any punishment just to be amongst his own folk on his native land. At last he said: 'Tell me, could they shoot me?'

'What for?'

'Well, I'm a Kulak [land-owning peasants persecuted by Stalin's regime – trans.]. I defected.'

'I don't think they'll punish you,' said I, 'you've been punished enough for what you've done.'

'I'm not afraid of punishment, I'll even ask them to punish me – then my conscience will be clear. I'll never forgive myself that I haven't returned before. But I believed all kinds of gossip and was scared. My mother, father and sisters are back there. Maybe they're still alive?'

At that moment someone yelled loudly in broken Russian: 'Is

Pogozhi Andrei, number 1418 here?' I shuddered as if from a blow of the whip. Noticing my reaction my countryman shrank away, his eyes shifting like those of a cornered animal: 'Is that you? What for?' he asked in a frightened whisper. A moment of bewilderment went by. I climbed down from the bunk and walked into the aisle. A big, solid, red-cheeked fellow in clean prison clothes stood before me: 'Are you number 1418?' – 'Yes.' Suddenly, Gurecki appeared as if from underground. He looked perfectly calm but I noticed a shadow of alarm flicker in his eyes: 'I'm the clerk of this room. Please be so kind as to explain what you need this patient for, if it's not a secret?' The big man smiled and answered in Polish: 'We lost this man. Birkenau registered him as dead but the crematorium hadn't confirmed it. I was doing reconciliation today and decided to clarify why a dead body wasn't cremated. But see how well he looks!' – 'Is *sir* joking?' Gurecki asked him with a smile in his voice. The giant boomed: 'Of course not! Now, sir, come on, show me your number. Right, it's 1418. That's fine. I'll move your registration card from the crematorium to the hospital. It happens rarely – usually it's the other way around! Good day, gentlemen . . .'

Next moment my countryman was running towards me, breathless with joy and looking at me with rapture: 'You'll live!' he cried, 'yes, it's the surest sign! Once you've been among the dead, you're sure to live . . .' I'm not superstitious but in my position how could I disbelieve this happy omen? A pleasant wave washed over my mind, heart and body. Was it really true? Would it really come to pass?

My countryman and I talked longer yet. We remembered the years of school and childhood. We remembered 1929 – the year neither of us could forget: tragic for him and happy for me. That year, at almost the same time, we left our native villages. He rushed overseas from Kuban and I left the banks of the Don to study. Here were two different lives and fates indeed.

Late that evening he left in a happier mood. But I lay awake, thinking about my comrades, my kinfolk, and my Motherland. How many times had life assured me of the correctness of the comparison between Motherland and the dear word 'mother'. While you live under your mother's careful guardianship you don't value it at its true worth. Sometimes it even seems that her actions hold you back. But as soon as you leave your mother, you begin to understand the weight of the loss – you start to appreciate all those things you hadn't even noticed before. And such is your Motherland. We live and remember her from time to time; we live and don't notice that she protects our lives and our comfort, that she looks after us like a loving mother looks after her kids, regardless of their age. But once you find yourself outside her borders the absence of her powerful influence begins to tell. I could understand the harshness of my countryman's footloose life. As an inexperienced youngster, finding himself in strange lands and being driven to despair, he'd turned into a stray animal that some feared and others ignored. Thus no one appreciated his spiritual tragedy. Anyone would have felt helpless in that jungle. I felt and understood his state of mind keenly, for my situation wasn't much different from his. Both of us had lost our Motherland, although in different ways, and were paying for it with our health and lives. The Motherland had turned into a dream for us: painfully remote and unreachable, but dearly longed-for nevertheless.

My countryman! My comrade! The deep meaning of this word could be understood only by someone who, by the will of fate, had suffered in a strange land far away from his Motherland, among people at the last stage of human degradation. A comrade means friendly help, support at a difficult moment, kind advice and constructive criticism after mistakes, understanding how you feel inside. It means shared ideas and shared dreams, without which it's impossible to withstand the blows of fate, the death and suffering of friends, or to overcome your own weakness at times of spiritual depression.

In May I accidentally discovered something shocking and monstrous in design. One day two prisoners with disfigured faces were brought to the hospital. One had a huge left ear – the lobe of it touched his shoulder – and the left half of his face was pulled downward under its weight, exposing the eyeball. The skull of the second man was strangely formed – the forehead low and the jawbone abnormally small, and because of this his face seemed to be flattened out. The serious and thoughtful expression in their eyes was at odds with their appearance. Upon entering, with a sad smile and a nod, they gave a friendly greeting to a patient lying on a bunk next to the aisle, who'd arrived in the hospital several days ago. The cordiality of the silent exchange showed that they knew each other well. After providing some kind of assistance or consultation, the deformed prisoners left with their escort.

In the evening of the same day, sweeping the room, I found myself next to the patient so warmly greeted by the deformed inmates. He appeared to be a sculptor of Yugoslavian nationality. I found out from our talk that there was an arts workshop in the camp, where prisoners – talented artists of various nationalities – worked. It turned out that, as soon as transports arrived, all those with physical defects – especially of the face and skull – were selected. Provided with better living conditions than other prisoners, their sculptural portraits were made and photographs taken in the workshop. Then, when the artists had finished their work, these people were liquidated or transferred to work crews and their sculptures sent to the Reich's ethnography museum, in order to expand the stock of displays confirming the Fascists' 'scientific' theory of Aryan superiority over other races.

At the beginning of June the General-Major was discharged. He and I parted like father and son. He was a good and courageous man. Since he was being sent to Birkenau we agreed that we would meet there. We made our farewells simply, expecting to meet again. Three days later the old man was murdered by an SS guard escorting prisoners. Limping and unable to keep up with the others, the General was killed in cold blood because he couldn't walk fast enough for the guard's liking.

By the end of June my wound had healed so well that no more dressings were applied, except for bands of sticking plasters. All my fingers moved obediently, thanks to the exercises Türschmidt had recommended.

The last day in the hospital. Several men had been discharged. All of them were to go to Birkenau. The farewell was touching. I made a round of all the patients in the hall and wished them a happy recovery, a quick liberation, and reunion with their families. I said farewell to each doctor individually. Gurecki and I hugged and kissed each other like brothers. I had grown fond of this good and modest man, to whom I was so much obliged. We parted forever, not hiding our tears.

CHAPTER SEVEN

Gallows

Early July 1942. Birkenau is meshed with barbed wire, giving it the appearance of a huge spider's web. I can see that a central road divides the camp in two. On the right sprawls a vast area under construction – the gouged ground ready for new drains and foundations. Meanwhile, prefabricated wooden huts stand already completed. On each of them shines a bright enamelled square containing large, black German script: 'Pferde Baracken' – 'Horse Barracks'. On the left of the road I see the entrance to the women's camp. Behind it, separated by barbed wire, is that of the men. In both these compounds big new structures have been built alongside the original brick barracks – they look just like the stables opposite. Now I look straight ahead: the only road crossing the camp from east to west terminates at a small grove immediately beyond its limits – the gas chambers and crematorium are situated there. This is the appearance of the Birkenau camp – 'Auschwitz II' – as our truck approaches. I am one of a large group of prisoners being driven from Central Auschwitz . . .

I suddenly found my head spinning with memories. During three months spent in the hospital the psychological wounds of the recent past had begun to heal: but they immediately opened again. Nothing had changed. Still the same horrifying brutality.

The Soviet POWs had been transferred from the brick barracks into a wooden stable. Out of the 600 survivors I left behind in March only 150 were still alive. Now Frenchmen had been lumped together with the Russians. Thus I was fated never to see many of my old comrades again. But to my great joy Viktor Kouznetsov and Pavel Sten'kin were still alive. But Pavlik was bleeding badly from wounds on his feet and could barely walk.

During the first days of my arrival at Birkenau, when I was still in the process of acclimatization after hospital, an event occurred that sickened all prisoners in the camp: the first public execution for an escape attempt.

The sultry July sun was shining. The air was hot and still. A suffocating silence – lunch break. Thousands of prisoners were sitting or lying under the cloudless sky, scattered like grain from a basket by some invisible hand. Even though no SS men or Kapos were around, no one was speaking or moving. Exhausted by beatings, starvation and heat, the prisoners – pathetic shadows of former human beings – were savouring a moment's rest, scared of missing a few seconds of their short break. The silence was broken by the beating of a gong: the break was over. The camp began to move like a huge anthill as prisoners got up from the ground and shuffled off in groups to the shouts of arriving Kapos and Vorarbeiters. With their heads drawn into their shoulders, bending under the weight of picks or shovels, the slaves set off for work, sluggish ones driven with sticks.

Cursing and yelling, the SS men came strutting. Smart, and with jackboots polished to a shine, the smug and self-satisfied butchers scrutinized everything that fell into their field of vision. Some prisoners passed out in the soaring heat – they were dragged like sacks into a pile. There they lay gulping for air, already crossed off the list of the living. Two Blockführers approached this heap of ruined humanity, contemptuously grimacing. Nearby, a Kapo, red-faced with zeal, yelled with all the strength of his lungs: 'Achtung! Mützen ab!' ('Attention! Caps off!'). Everyone around stood rooted to the spot, heads bare. Only those writhing in the pile kept moving – minds dead but bodies still alive. Scowling at the people standing around, one of the Blockführers barked out:

'Weiter machen!' ('Carry on!') and the bystanders got down to their hated work, under the blows of the Kapo's fist.

In the meantime another SS-Mann, having taken a few steps, stopped next to a spread-eagled wretch making futile attempts to sit up. With a practised swipe of his steel-capped jackboot the brute silenced him for good: 'Kaput!' he pronounced with a grin. For a few seconds he stared in silence at the man at his feet, who lay on his back, staring at the sky through a foggy gaze, understanding nothing as his mouth worked soundlessly and his fingers scraped at the soil. The SS-Mann kicked his head like a football, smashing the skull at the temple: 'Schwein!' Having fastidiously wiped his bloody boot on the lifeless body, the SS-Mann pulled out a cigarette-case and calmly lit up.

Suddenly a siren howled, swelling in volume and sharpening in pitch. The SS men, letting forth a stream of oaths, strode towards the main gate of the camp. Their leader knocked down the first prisoner he came across – some hapless slave who'd respectfully doffed his cap and stood aside. Wiping the blood from his nose, the battered prisoner sat up, traced the siren-sounds to their source with his eyes and . . . smiled. All around people froze: some with joy, some with alarm, some with anger. For the screeching siren – filling the air with metallic shrieks – was notifying the whole area that someone had escaped.

Escape! How much hope, anxiety, joy and emotion this word contained. Escape was the secret dream of the death camp prisoners. Escape offered a chance of survival. Escape meant freedom or death. Despite humiliation, starvation, torture and relentless psychological stress, the thought of escape had never left the most bold-spirited prisoners. And the cruelly refined punishments that attended failure did not deter those who were unafraid of an agonizing death.

The siren continued to howl, alerting the camp and its surroundings: 'An escape! An escape!' But how many were on the run? And who were they – Poles, Russians, Czechs, French, Jews, Slovaks, Germans? And where could they be? During daylight not even a hare could run unnoticed through the dense chain of SS guard posts. They must be hiding somewhere, in order to get away under cover of night. Will the guards find them? Maybe, they already have . . .

And when the siren eventually fell silent – like the moans of a man dying from a poison injection – a message was passed from mouth to mouth: some Russians had escaped, three of them. Neither the shouts nor the sticks of the Kapos and Vorarbeiters could make the prisoners work now: instead they wandered about, gathering in groups, discussing only one thing – the Russians escaped! Will they find them or not? And their heads involuntary turned East. Eyes full of tears and hope looked towards the place where millions were fighting for life, freedom, justice – the place where the fate of the enslaved peoples of Europe was being decided. Yes, the symbol of the East burned with hope, while that of the West remained in shade. Over there, out of the forest situated near the camp, puffs of black smoke were rising – the smoke of huge pyres, in which thousands of corpses of gassed women, old men and children were burning. The smoke, as if ashamed of its origin, refused to rise to heaven: instead it drifted west, covering the living with the dead – countless particles of people converted into smoke and ash. And while a cannonade and powerful, all-shattering anthem of victory were heard in our imaginations from the East, hysterical screams, children's sobs and shots were heard from the forest to the West.

The working day was over, the heat less oppressive. Prisoners began moving more energetically. A relatively quiet night was coming, heralded by the beats of the gong. Suddenly the opening bars of a march struck up, played by a symphony orchestra comprising over 100 musicians. Once the pride of acclaimed conservatoria, these skeletal, striped-suited virtuosi now strained every nerve to extract from their instruments sounds to refresh the stuffy atmosphere of the camp. Meanwhile, the column of prisoners filed past, carrying dead and dying comrades on their shoulders like some returning legion of antiquity.

Evening roll-call. The Russians had seemingly disappeared without trace. Even a pack of German Shepherd dogs, having scoured the whole camp, found no trace of the courageous men. The prisoners sighed with relief. But next morning, immediately after reveille, everyone was stunned to hear that the escapees were in the bunker . . .

Several days went by. During lunch break all the work crews were lined up and led in one direction: towards a square near the kitchen. Many thousands gathered and everyone was perplexed: what was going on? A heavy machine-gun had been set up in front of the gate, the external guard reinforced with submachine-gunners. And then we saw the gallows. A crowd of Kapos and SS men approached it with a ladder and stools. They quickly installed the ladder and began tying ropes with nooses onto the crossbar. One of the SS men stood up on a stool and, laughing, tested the length of the rope on himself . . .

Hearing shouts, the line of prisoners stepped apart. A covered truck drove up. Three staggering prisoners with swollen faces covered in bruises were led out of it, hands tied behind their backs with wire. With difficulty, some among the crowd recognized the condemned men as comrades, but unfortunately my memory failed to retain their names.

'Achtung! Mützen ab!' The Camp Commandant and his retinue arrived in two light vehicles. One of the officers began yelling something in German, roaring in a staccato voice and pointing at the three Soviet POWs. When he finally stopped, an interpreter piped up: 'For infringement of discipline, an attempt to escape, the court decrees . . .'

'Butchers! Murderers!' shouted one of the condemned men, raising his head. The crowd of prisoners swarmed and buzzed like a startled colony of bees. The Lagerführer waved his hand. Several SS men and Kapos rushed towards the Russians and knocking them over, began stuffing their caps in their mouths. Next moment our comrades were bundled onto the stools and nooses were placed round their necks. And yet they remained calm as the butchers bustled around them, looking with bulging eyes for their comrades and friends in the crowd, the filthy gags sticking out of their mouths.

Meanwhile, the Lagerführers seemed strangely animated by the spectacle, talking and laughing the whole time. But the prisoners stood with lowered heads. Many wept. In our hearts burned a raging thirst for revenge. Suddenly, one of the condemned men, gathering all his nerve, spat out his gag: 'Curse you, you butchers! Escape! Tell everyone . . .' A Kapo rushed at him – but he lifted his foot and kicked the brute in the face. This sudden effort caused the condemned man to lose balance: the stool tilted from under his feet and the noose tightened round his throat. Thus the man was launched into eternity, having managed to cry: 'Farewell, comrades!'

The other stools were immediately kicked over and a convulsive shuddering of instantly-stretched bodies followed. All the prisoners removed their caps as if by order. An agonized silence fell. The ropes slowly twisted back and forth, as if deliberately displaying the blue-faced corpses, hands still bound with wire, clenched and covered with blood.

After the execution the SS men, apparently in compliance with some order, began behaving especially brutally. Their henchmen – the Kapos and Vorarbeiters – obsequiously copied them. From morning to evening the SS men strutted about the camp tormenting prisoners and carping at the tiniest infringements of regulations. Only night would free us from suffering.

When night fell the only gateway to the camp was secured. Then the Kapos and Vorarbeiters locked themselves inside a separate barracks and silence reigned. During the hours of darkness prisoners flit like shadows through the blacked-out camp (only the outer fence was brightly lit), some driven by the call of nature, others raving with lunatic fantasies.

Actually, one building was illuminated at night, but nothing would induce prisoners to go near it. This place was Block 7 or 'Sedemka', as it was called by everyone in Polish [more correctly 'siódemka', meaning 'seventh' – trans.]. A brick barracks hugging the ground – similar to the one in which the first Soviet POWs were accommodated in March – this structure had an enclosed inner yard like that between Blocks 10 and 11 of the central camp. Sedemka was the gateway to the gas chambers.

Prisoners were placed in this gloomy barracks after morning and evening roll-calls. These were the ones who, due to their physical condition, were unable to work, and who'd been refused medical treatment by the SS men, the Blockführers, or the Chief Doctor of the camp hospital. They were joined by all prisoners who showed signs of mental illness, as well as those awaiting punishment. Their fate depended on the head of Sedemka and his assistants. Every day the fit, well-fed sadists would personally select prisoners for the gas chambers – not only terminally ill patients but also healthy men who, for some reason, they simply didn't like. The only survivors in Sedemka were those who managed to keep out of the monsters' way or who cringed and fawned before them. All prisoners avoided Sedemka, which stank of excrement and suppurating wounds. A chaotic buzz was usually heard from the inner yard, illuminated at night by lights hanging from brackets above. Then we'd hear cries for help, moans, curses, singing, sobbing . . .

Very few returned from Sedemka. Thus only one Soviet POW came back – he was just lucky. I remember him very well before he went to Sedemka: a short man with narrow shoulders and a mild blue-eyed gaze. He was no different from his comrades and always tried to be quiet and anonymous. But whether he thought of it himself, or someone suggested the idea to him, he suddenly began telling fortunes. A nickname immediately stuck to him: 'Ivan the Fortune Teller'. As he was the only one of this kind in the camp, prisoners of all nationalities came to him. Mostly they were deeply religious people who had no doubt of his 'gift'.

Once an ageing grey-haired SS-Mann came into the block we were in. At the order 'Achtung!' we froze as the Blockältester rushed up to him. The SS-Mann walked along the bunks silently, scrutinizing everyone with an openly hostile stare, then suddenly ordered in quite pure Russian: 'At ease!' It turned out that he was a former White Guard, a noble from St Petersburg. Even his manner of speech gave away the fact that he was an ardent enemy of Soviet Russia. 'Is there someone from St Petersburg here?' he asked. 'I'm from Leningrad . . .' someone answered ingenuously, referring to the city's Soviet name. 'I'm asking about St Petersburg, bastard!' said the SS-Mann. The situation had taken a turn for the worse, so all further questions were answered with a 'yes', 'no', or 'don't know'. The SS-Mann turned to the Blockältester, standing stiffly to attention, and began talking with him in German. A few minutes later the Blockältester called Ivan the Fortune Teller. The SS-Mann extended his right hand, turned it palm-up, and with spite still in his voice, asked: 'What's in store for me?' Terrified and pale, Ivan stared stupidly at the large, pink palm. Losing patience, the former White Guard yelled: 'Tell my fortune!' Understanding that it was too late to retreat, Ivan put his hands together on his chest, as if in prayer, raised his eyes towards the ceiling and began to talk. The essence of his prophecy was that the man would receive an unpleasant message from home but would live in good health to a very old age.

Generally speaking, Ivan was no fool, and was obviously crafty: whether there was a letter or not, in time of war one would rarely get cheerful news from home, and Ivan's prophecies could be applied to any occasion. But this encounter ended tragically for the fortune teller. In a day or two the SS-Mann really did receive unpleasant news from home and ordered Ivan to be punished with twenty-five lashes and sent to Sedemka. Fortunately for Ivan, he came across one of his old clients in Sedemka, a man for whom he'd foretold something successfully once upon a time. This man helped Ivan recover from the flogging and eventually to return to the camp.

Strangely enough, among the SS men serving in the camp were a few relatively decent people. Back then there was barely anyone among us who didn't know one of this kind, and wasn't happy to have come across him.

From some Ukrainians who worked in the camp's food stock-room we heard for the first time about a strange SS-Mann. A prisoner native to the Western Ukraine ran the stockroom. At his request a permanent crew of three or four people consisting of his countrymen, Soviet POWs, had been assigned to assist him. Once, during an evening roll-call, they told us about an unusual event that had happened that day.

In the middle of the day a soldier in SS uniform entered the storeroom. No one had seen him before. The storekeeper wasn't around, but when his deputy shouted 'Achtung!' the SS-Mann simply waved his hand, and paying no attention to the prisoners, who were busy with cleaning, silently walked up to a shelf, cut a slice of bread and some blood-pudding, and began a leisurely meal. The first sandwich was soon followed by another: it was clear the man was hungry. One of the prisoners, pretending to fix his broom and confident the SS-Mann wouldn't understand him, quietly said in Russian: 'Look at him feasting! He's eating as if it's his!' The SS-Mann suddenly turned to him, and without raising his voice asked: 'You begrudge it?' Overwhelmed, the prisoners held their breath, expecting retribution. But the SS-Mann returned to his chewing as though nothing had happened. Having finished his impromptu meal, the newcomer shook the breadcrumbs off his tunic, glanced at his watch, and unhurriedly walked towards the exit: 'Here we go, chaps!' he said from the door, smiling slightly.

During the roll-call we all saw this SS-Mann. He entered the camp in a column of Blockführers. He carried out roll-call for the Polish blocks located next to us. He was middle-aged, a bit stooping. The way he walked – in fact all his movements – bespoke an exceptionally calm and even-tempered character. When watching him one might conclude that he was doing every-thing extremely unwillingly. Even when reporting the results of the roll-call to a Schreiberführer – while other SS men would hurry, almost running – he would only increase his pace and, somewhat absurdly, throw his back his head. After the roll-call, when the Lagerführer and his retinue had left, he came up to the barracks where the Soviet POWs lived: 'Greetings, chaps!' he said in Russian to a group of prisoners standing near the gate. He pronounced the Russian words distinctly but with difficulty, mangling stress. He tried to strike up a conversation, but having learned from bitter experience to fear a trap, we gave him disjointed answers only: 'Yes', 'No', 'Of course', 'That would be fine', the abrupt answers resounded. But the SS-Mann managed to win over the whole lot of us with his composure, his clever eyes, and his earnest questions, for it was obvious that he found himself in such a camp for the first time. After about thirty minutes he left, smiling warmly and cordially: 'Good day chaps!'

Over the following days, the new Blockführer – immediately nicknamed 'Chaps' – would frequently come to our barracks and our relations with him improved with each visit. He treated the Soviet people with an unconcealed sympathy that was especially obvious when there were no outside witnesses. He tried to cheer us up with jokes and vital hints, to keep up the spirits of those who were losing hope of salvation. He knew and loved Russian proverbs, the wisdom of which he understood subtly, but he sometimes distorted them to the point of absurdity: 'Those who know not are helped by God!' was his translation of 'Rely on God but don't slip up yourself!' Initially we thought that he was worming himself into our confidence, but the more we learned about him the more we trusted him. 'I understand everything in Russian when I read it,' he admitted with a smile, 'and when it's not spoken quickly . . .'

Once 'Chaps' found out that one of our comrades – a sick man – had been beaten by a Vorarbeiter. 'Chaps' asked us to secretly show him that man. No one knew what occurred between them but the Vorarbeiter – a German criminal and thorough scoundrel – was apparently replaced.

'Chaps' came almost daily, bringing saccharin and cigarettes. But his most valuable gift was information, which took the form of hints and warnings. If a stranger had overheard, he'd have taken these words for jokes or ironic remarks. But we'd catch their meaning immediately. For example, one evening we were all stripped naked and ordered to hand over our clothes, as if for disinfection. 'Chaps' came around and casually said: 'By the way, guys, it would be good if you kept your eye on Brama during the night. Just in case . . .' Straight away lookouts were organized. We made arrangements with a Pole who was in charge of the clothes storeroom, located in one of the deserted barracks, that if there was an alarm he'd be tied up to divert suspicion from him and the clothes would be taken back. The Pole showed us where all the stuff lay. Few of us slept that night but nothing happened. The clothes were returned next morning. But our fears were not unfounded: an action had been planned but something had prevented its implementation.

Many such warnings helped save the lives of Soviet POWs. Meanwhile, the knowledge that a friend could help in a moment of danger gave us strength and faith in the future, instilling hope of salvation.

CHAPTER EIGHT

Sonderkommandos

The word 'Auschwitz' aroused fear and horror in all who heard it – even those who'd never entered its gates. We were made aware of this by questioning those who'd just been imprisoned. Most of them hadn't even known what was *really* happening in this Polish town, but fear had arisen from the grains of truth, sometimes absurdly distorted, leaking through the reinforced chain of guards, through the web of high-voltage barbed wire, and out across the wastelands and bogs.

Those who came to make up the numbers in the camp, having undergone a fitness check on arrival, fell into one of two categories on their very first day, depending on their psychological condition. The first category – most numerous by far – consisted of those who couldn't stomach the reality of all they saw and heard. Their nerves failed, they lost their minds, they committed suicide. Losing all hope of salvation and becoming physically and spiritually weak, they perished from beatings, torture, sickness and starvation. Their life expectancy in the camp could be numbered in days. The second category consisted of stronger spirits. Finding the courage to get over the tragic deaths of kinfolk and comrades, they became acclimatized to the savage living conditions in the camp. Most retained their humanity. Thus, friendly assistance and support – regardless of age or nationality – exerted a positive influence on a prisoner's life, which was hidden from the guards, the administration, and their agents – both overt and covert.

There were quite a few prisoners in the camp who'd been there several months, or even more than a year. Very many of them had, without staining their consciences, survived the shock of the first horrible days, and later would try to take more cold-bloodedly the terrible crimes to which they were unwilling witnesses on a daily basis. They didn't lack natural instincts like fear or the desire for self-preservation: but having become deadened by the grim conditions of the camp, only the activities of certain work crews could bring them out. I'm talking about the penal crews or 'Sonderkommandos'. The disgusting work of these 'Special Units' caused all prisoners to avoid them. In fact, socializing with their members was forbidden. They were the unluckiest crews in Birkenau, and those who ended up in them were strictly segregated from all others.

The first Sonderkommando was formed at the end of 1941. It dug pits and carried out mass burials of bodies which, for some reason, hadn't been taken to the crematorium. The burials were done in Birkenau. The second Sonderkommando was formed in March 1942. The men of the Sonderkommandos lived in isolation in the main camp, so no one could tell what they were doing in the forest, which grew right up to the camp grounds on its north-western side. This secrecy led to the most incredible rumours – many of them contradictory. Even we, who'd grown used to extremities, couldn't believe these horror stories. Some rumours reached my ears when I was in the hospital, and there we had even less idea what was going on in Birkenau.

On my return to Birkenau I'd been placed in the 'Wascherei' crew – in the washhouse. My duty was to hang out linen to dry after washing. The washhouse was situated in the south-western corner of the men's camp, and watching over the drying linen I could see the adjacent grove. There, hidden behind the trees, I could make out silhouettes of people and the outline of a building. Black puffs of smoke – sometimes with bright tongues of fire – rose from this wooded area behind the camp day and night, dissipating in the air or settling on the ground as a grey coating. We nicknamed this place where pyres were burning the 'Secret Village' or 'Secret Grove'.

At the end of July 1942 (or the beginning of August) both Sonderkommandos were merged and transferred to permanent accommodation in Birkenau. They were allocated a separate barracks-stable next to the fence. One end of the barracks was boarded up, the other faced a watch tower with an SS guard. Two men were chosen from the Soviet POWs for around-the-clock guard duty at the Sonderkommando barracks. To my great surprise one of those two happened to be myself. We were under the orders of the senior 'Sonderführer'. This SS officer – with his short legs, massive shoulders, crimson face, and small spiteful eyes – was aptly nicknamed 'the Bull'. An Iron Cross dangled below his fatty double-chin. Under threat of being shot or transferred to a penal crew, we were banned from talking to members of the Sonderkommando, with the exception of the Kapo – a prisoner acting as overseer. Meanwhile, when walking to and from their barracks, the Sonderkommando men – including the Kapo himself – were supposed to keep within an established zone, running 5 metres from the barracks, and were forbidden to socialize with other prisoners. The guard on the watch tower was charged with checking that.

After a few days, in spite of the strict prohibition, we – and not only we – knew at first-hand what was happening in the 'Secret Grove' behind the camp; knew what the Sonderkommandos were doing and who was involved. The rumours were fully confirmed. One Sonderkommando – more numerous than the other – dug pits for mass graves – burying the evidence from pyres, gas chambers and crematoria. The other one serviced the first gas chamber, which was set up like a bath-house. Corpses were burned in the crematoria and on pyres. Everyone in the crew had his duties clearly spelled out. Each man knew what he was meant to be doing. And no corpse would be burned (either in the crematorium or on the pyres) unless it had undergone a thorough examination. For example, specially assigned 'dentists' from among the doctor-prisoners would examine the mouths of corpses. Dental crowns and plates would be torn out under the supervision of the Sonderführer and stockpiled in special crates. Earrings and bracelets would go in as well. In order to remove rings, fingers often had to be chopped off.

The unification of the two Sonderkommandos, and their move to Birkenau, had been forced by circumstances. Some time prior to that a putrid smell of such power had appeared over the area of Sonderkommando activities that even the German Shepherd dogs couldn't stand it. This stench had reached the camp but we couldn't understand where it was coming from. It turned out that the land had subsided above huge mass graves, previously known only to the Sonderkommandos. Neither chloride of lime nor any other chemical helped. Fetid ponds formed over the graves and it became impossible for the Sonderkommandos to work. Even the SS men were walking around in gas masks. An order arrived to clean up the graves and burn the remains. The joint Sonderkommando was divided into two for rostered around-the-clock work. After coming back from work the first crew would stop near the barracks to take off their special issue gumboots, trousers and jackets, which stank so sickeningly. Then the second crew would don these clothes and go to work. The escort accompanying these crews was increased. Several German Shepherd dogs were with them all the time.

Meanwhile, huge pyres burned next to the graves. Remains were taken out with long hooks and burned up straight away. The workers were issued with vodka and they did their job half-drunk. Every day the crews got replacements because many couldn't stand it: they'd lose their minds, commit suicide. There were cases of assaults on the guards and Sonderführers. The attackers were shot on the spot. Several prisoners from the labour crews threw themselves into the raging flames of the pyres.

We quickly got acquainted with the Sonderkommandos and established good relations, not only with the Kapos of the teams, Weiss and Goldberg, but also with many ordinary crew members, who knew Polish and Russian. It became clear from their stories that there were remains of Soviet POWs in the graves. This was shocking news. Who were they? Maybe they were those comrades who'd been transported to the camp before us and gassed in the basement of Block 11? After all, they'd not been burned in the crematorium. Jackboots, buttons, belts, field caps, flasks, mess tins, confirmed without question their membership of the Soviet Army. The stuff also confirmed that they'd not been taken from the transports that had brought us down here, for we'd been forced to undress – none of us even had a flask or a mess tin. Someone from the crew dredged up a plastic ID cartridge by chance [in the Soviet Army servicemen carried their identity information in plastic cartridges – trans.]. It was possible to make out several letters on a piece of paper covered with brown-yellow spots: 'Col . . . An . . .' – obviously, 'Colonel An . . .'

In five or six days pyres began blazing over the place of former graves and the Sonderkommandos set about their main jobs. During this period their ranks had been almost completely renewed, but both Kapos and about ten men were still alive from the original crew. They described themselves as men without hearts or nerves – brutalized beings in whom the instinct of self-preservation had, if not yet wiped out their human feelings, at least driven them to the lowermost level.

Meanwhile the Sonderkommando barracks reminded one of a psychiatric clinic: there were always raving lunatics in it. They'd be tied up by their own comrades every evening and sent to Sedemka after roll-call. The quieter lunatics would wait for evening hidden in a corner; others paced around the barracks or spent their time singing, dancing, praying, crying, laughing. Their comrades simply got used to their presence, as to an inevitable necessity, and no one paid any attention to them. Those with suicidal intentions could be identified by their agitated condition. Their comrades would do their best to calm them down and talk them out of it. Many had become sick, reduced to physical wrecks. But Sonderkommando prisoners were deprived of medical help – even by camp standards – so invalids were simply shifted down to the lower bunks of the barrack. Periodically the Bull would conduct a fitness check on the crew. The frequency of fitness checks depended on the number of sick: for there had to be the maximum number capable of work in the crew every day. Those who failed the fitness check would be sent to Sedemka for extermination.

The Bull was remarkable for his bestial cruelty. The most difficult shift for the Sonderkommando would be the one for which he was the supervising SS official. Any expression of weakness or human emotion – even when encountering the corpse of one's gassed father, mother, brother, sister or children – meant execution on the spot. The Bull could calmly shoot without a tremor of his hand even the moving body of an infant, convulsively pressed against the breast of its dead mother.

Here was an astonishing puzzle! We'd heard stories from Sonderkommando crewmen about how the gas dosage used for mass extermination – fatal for adults – sometimes failed to kill babies. Indeed, the younger they were, the more signs of life these infants displayed: they'd lose their voice and move their arms and legs soundlessly. The Bull could calmly finish those kids off with his pistol. There were cases when he and another SS-Mann took kids by the legs and threw them into the flames of a pyre. Few could witness this kind of sadism and remain sane.

Once a remarkable incident befell the Bull, showing that deep inside the mean soul of this foul Fascist – and moreover inside the other 'craftsmen' of the death factory – lurked hidden fear. The Kapo of the first crew – 'Kapo Number One' as he was usually called – was the first to tell about it . . .

It was early morning. The newborn sun was still hidden behind the wall of the Secret Grove but its beams were already shining through the trees, fragmented by the leaves into a countless number of dancing flashes, which enlivened the gloomy landscape of the clearing. Surrounded by a fence of dense barbed wire, here Death was master. Traces of His work were seen on the ground: the grey ashes of burned people, trees blackened with soot from the pyres, the heavy and stinking air spreading over the grove. In contrast to this gloomy scene were several neat lawns with lush greenery, in the midst of which flowers stood out with their many-coloured hues: the sentimental caprice of one of the butchers.

Through the doors of the gas chamber – wide open for airing and work – above the pediment of which a signboard with large letters 'Bath-house' caught one's eye, one could see a chaotic pile of corpses. Dozens of women and children were frozen in the most incredible postures of mortal agony. It was the latest party from a transport that had arrived the day before from France. The Sonderkommando, exhausted during the night, was working in a hurry. The Bull entered the gas chamber with his hands behind his back, his piggish eyes seeing and noticing everything. The holster of his pistol was unfastened as usual, a German Shepherd bitch following closely at his heels. The dog wouldn't walk around the corpses but calmly stepped over them, keeping a professional eye on all the movements of the prisoners. Her pricked-up ears twitched nervously, catching all unaccustomed sounds. The SS beast slid his eyes over a familiar picture: a baby with plump, rounded arms and legs and a curly shock of blond hair lay on his belly in a frozen posture of crawling forward. His mother lay half a metre away with outstretched arms. Her hands and face expressed the suffering of her soul and her last conscious thoughts, full of alarm and agony for the son crawling away from her arms. The Bull grimaced contemptuously, looking into the dull, glassy eyes of an ageing woman with crimson bruises on her face.

Suddenly he stopped, examining the corpse of a stunningly beautiful girl, laying face up. Her right arm was tossed aside, the left was covering her breasts, as if she were ashamed. A fringe of eyelashes edged her closed eyelids. Her eyebrows were elegantly curved. A gleam shone from the even row of beautiful teeth showing in her half-opened mouth, her pink lips giving the pale face an especially tender expression. Several ringlets of fluffy chestnut hair had broken loose from her fancy hairdo, disturbed by the draught caressing her high, bare forehead. One couldn't believe she was dead. One didn't want to believe that she would never again open her eyes, smile and speak. The Sonderführer stared at her as if hypnotized. The German Shepherd looked devotedly at him. 'Kapo!' the hoarse muffled voice of the Bull resounded, 'lift her up and follow me. Pick some flowers!' and he walked towards the exit.

The astounded Sonderkommando men stopped work, staring at the bent back of their Sonderführer. In a few minutes green branches and bright flowers were put around the corpse of the unknown girl, which was set against the external wall of the gas chamber. As if sneaking up, the blood-red disc of the sun rose from behind the trees, pouring its beams on the horrible scene, where the subdued Sonderführer, the Kapo, and the whole Sonderkommando crew stood holding their breath, looking at the dead girl framed with live flowers. An agonizing silence fell. Tears flowed down the dirty, distorted faces of the prisoners. The Bull breathed heavily. 'Kapo!' he shouted in agitation, 'we think no one knows about it, but they do! They do! And we'll have to answer for it all . . .'

Suddenly a bloodcurdling yell was heard. With a hysterical howl, one of the Sonderkommando men fell into a seizure, squirming next to the dead girl, tearing his face with his hands till it bled. The moaning and sobbing merged into a whine. Coming to his senses the Bull – grown crimson with bloodshot eyes ready to leap out of their sockets – turned abruptly, pulling out his pistol: 'Get away!' he yelled. 'Get away, you rogues!' Shots burst through the silence of the dawning day. He shot one bullet after another into the writhing madman until a metallic click declared the chamber empty. The German Shepherd howled quietly, unable to understand the state of her master's soul. Kicking the dog with his jackboot, the Bull entered the gas chamber with fury on his face, the pistol still in his hand. The Sonderkommando resumed work at a run, each prisoner afraid of drawing the attention of their terrifying master: for attention meant death.

Meanwhile, even prettier in the rays of the risen sun, the unknown girl from France – whose blossoming life had been cut short so cruelly – was left forlorn. And what for? What kind of crime did she commit . . . ?

With my eyes closed I can still hear the Kapo's voice – yes, what kind of crime did she commit? The Kapo repeated his question in a hissing, sinister voice. His neck extended, he was staring at me with rounded eyes burning with madness. I was astounded. Always calm and unruffled, he was unrecognizable. And his previous statement – that he and his Sonderkommando comrades had no heart or nerves; that they'd lost their humanity, save for outward appearance – seemed absurd. No, it was far away from being so. And as if to confirm it, he said: 'I've been considering your proposal. And the more I think about it, the more attractive it seems.' And with that the Kapo suddenly stood up and strode away, the silhouette of his stooping figure vanishing in the dark.

Kapo Number One was a good-looking middle-aged man. Tall, handsome, clever, he was a sober-minded individual who well understood the tragic nature of his situation, and that of his whole crew. And yet he remained surprisingly self-possessed. I knew that he was religious and prone to superstition: perhaps it was some inner faith that held his nerves together?

We'd made it a custom to run frank conversations in the evenings and nights. The camp would be submerged in gloomy sleep, while a line of smouldering cigarettes – like so many glow-worms – stretched along the Sonderkommando barracks wall, on the opposite side of the watch tower. The Sonderführer's instructions didn't operate at night but other regulations – the camp ones – were observed strictly: not to talk loudly, not to step into illuminated places, to smoke only in places invisible to the watchmen.

It was always crowded near the Sonderkommando barracks. People would come around to smoke, to talk to friends and acquaintances. They also came to find out news. After all, the Sonderkommando had not been only dragging gassed people from chambers and burning corpses, they'd also been carrying away the clothes of victims: hence they had some opportunity to discover what was happening outside the camp from overheard conversations, shreds of newspapers, notes and letters. What didn't we talk

[123]

about! People would gather in small groups. But in our group, without fail, there would always be Kapo Number One and his comrades from the crew. Once, the Kapo began a conversation like this:

'We can't expect or even cherish a tiny hope for salvation because we're firmly convinced that the Sonderkommando will be wiped out. They'll do their best to finish off those few who've been in it almost from the very beginning. We've seen too much, we know too much. I often think about my fate and you know, more and more, I get stuck on one idiotic idea, which has been tormenting and scaring me, like a sign that my mind is going. Not only I, but many others, cherish a hope that something super-natural is about to happen: someone will descend from the skies, pick us up under his wings and fly us away from this place, cursed by God and people. Weird, isn't it? But we're waiting. Yes, we are. Not literally, of course. But we're hoping for it. No one can live without hope . . .'

And then someone told him about our cherished thought, our deeply hidden dream:

'Between us, Kapo, when you're thinking about your fate, consider this proposal: is there any chance of catching a con-venient moment over there in the grove to knock off the SS men and get away? Be honest, have you never thought about it?'

After long silence Kapo Number One admitted: 'No, I haven't . . .'

That was the very proposal he was referring to after the incident with the unknown girl from France (in October 1944 the Sonderkommando of one crematorium would mutiny, slaying the guards and setting the crematorium ablaze. Was anyone from Kapo Number One's team in this rebellious crew? Did he live to see the rebellion? I'd like to think our frank conversations back then weren't in vain and we'd had a minor hand in that revolt – and of course, the beautiful French girl played her part). Stricken with the power and sincerity of the Kapo's outburst, we silently sat for a long time, reproducing in our minds the tragic scenario he'd just described. The whole camp gradually submerged into a sickly, nightmare-disturbed sleep. The first Sonderkommando, which had just come off shift, was falling asleep too. The glow-worms of cigarettes were dying away. Prisoners were disappearing in the dark like ghosts. Fatigue and the necessity of saving our strength forced people to disperse to their barracks.

Heniek [a variation of 'Henryk' – trans.], the Polish duty electrician, and I whiled away the time. Heniek was an excellent comrade. I'd known him since my first day after coming back to Birkenau. Once, when talking to him, I expressed in passing my surprise at how I – who'd been driven here from the central camp hospital essentially crippled, with an almost disabled hand – had been selected by a sadistic Blockältester for duty with the orderly team: after all, it was the most perilous crew in the camp. I remember how Heniek grinned. 'Someone,' he told me, 'suggested to the Blockältester to direct you here and he didn't dare disobey because he feared them more than the SS-Mann. Over here a man is needed who can be trusted and you'd earned this trust back in the hospital. Remember, you handed me a note from the hospital? It wasn't a letter to a relative – it was a good reference . . .' I was taken aback. I stood up, opened my mouth, and goggled at him. I probably had the most stupid expression on my face, and was later glad he probably couldn't see it in the dark. Taking advantage of my silence, Heniek shook my hand, clapped me on the shoulder, and vanished like the others.

Stifling heavy air saturated with sweat and fumes was radiating from the wide-open gates of the Sonderkommando barracks. Moaning, screaming, sobs were coming from inside. It was the usual nightmarish sleep of the exhausted prisoners. Their bodies could rest but their minds, never.

Late evening and night were the quietest times in Birkenau. More than an hour had already gone since the last SS man, the Sonderführer, had left the camp precincts. Now nerves were less strained, and after the meagre evening ration, the hunger pangs in our bellies less sharp. The silence and refreshing coolness of the night, the dome of the sky with the narrow sickle of the moon and shimmering scattering of stars, the quiet confidence that there was no danger around – all this disposed one to submerge into a world of fantasy, closing one's eyes and forgetting about the surrounding reality. Mesmerized by fantasies, in which all the humiliations, torments, tortures, deaths, were ruthlessly avenged, the brain grows quieter and begins to work in another direction . . .

My thoughts are far, far away. They drag me into the beloved past, skipping from one recollection to another with unimaginable speed. Events and episodes emerge from my memory, acquiring a new and deeper significance. My heart shrinks painfully, it becomes difficult to breathe. But then comes an unusual sensation of lightness in my body, my heart beats faster, a pleasant warmth relaxes my limbs, my lips stretch into a smile . . .

I suddenly wake up and, opening my eyes, come back to bitter reality. The thought of what I am, and where I am, pierces my soul with an acute pain, like a lightning strike. Cold sweat covers my body. I feel tingles down my back. No, no! I can't succumb to momentary weaknesses, no matter how pleasant and dear they are. The awakening affects my mind too badly. I must not forget that it's not a robust healthy body but my concentrated will that links me with life. It and only it maintains my strength, sharpening my senses to the limit, keeping my weak body safe from all deadly surprises. Only my will, like a fine thread, holds me over the yawning abyss of death.

CHAPTER NINE

Escape

In the summer of 1942 work on an extension to the camp began. An area several times larger than the original compound was laid out, opposite the existing men's and women's camps. Concrete walls and barbed wire were installed, new barracks were erected. Thousands of prisoners were employed on this project, including several Soviet work crews: although, by this time, only 130 of my countrymen remained alive.

Day-by-day columns of prisoners moved along the road from Auschwitz train station, which ran between the operating camp blocks and the ones under construction. Among the prisoners were people of all ages and nationalities. The columns always walked in the same direction: towards the gas chambers. There was no way back . . .

Meanwhile, the crematorium burned around the clock and huge pyres blazed. Black, choking smoke enveloped the camp, hampering breathing. Everything – the watch towers along the fence, the trained guard dogs, the monstrous ovens vomiting smoke – spoke of just one thing: death. But in spite of all, the dream of freedom lived in prisoners' minds. The boldest had been trying to escape with the resolution of the doomed, but their attempts ended tragically. Few – very few – managed to get away. And rarely would any of those who were caught survive. They'd be punished brutally: beaten to death before the whole camp. Any who – by some miracle – survived this treatment, would be finished off in the penal barracks.

The Soviet POWs stood out from the general mass on account of their special self-control. By all appearances they'd submitted to their fate, being diligent and disciplined in their work. But this was only a protective disguise. It deceived not only the camp administration but also its faithful watchdogs, the Kapos and Blockältesters. In reality, Soviet POWs were constantly thinking about escape as a way of struggling against the camp's tyranny. Despite anxiety caused by the intense desire to escape, the behaviour of the Soviet POWs didn't give away this determination. To the uninitiated it seemed that nothing untoward was going on: camp regulations were strictly observed, so there was no external sign of an impending explosion. And for the camp administration, the guards, and the majority of prisoners of other nationalities, escape seemed so unlikely that almost no one took the possibility seriously. For this reason talk of escape, when overheard, caused little alarm.

Meanwhile the camp continued to live by the established regulations. And the prisoners continued to die, fall sick, go mad, and commit suicide. And amidst the nightmare one could hear jokes, laughter and songs – one might even see lively dancing to a mouth-organ. This may seem strange and unreal, but that's how it was. It was necessary. There was a need for it – as for air, water and food – for all who didn't want to die, who retained a belief in Life while captive in the empire of Death.

Especially popular were the verbal retelling of novels, humorous stories, anecdotes and fables. They would transport you to a different world, help you forget the surrounding reality for a while. I suppose that stories like 'Pluck Flowers While They Bloom' – a heroic epic from the life of circus artists, or 'The Return' – the tale of a soldier who'd been through ordeals like ours and come back home, will linger in the memories of those who survived the camp. These stories not only distracted us, but also heightened morale, instilling courage and strengthening faith. A story from the life of the artilleryman, Sasha Sazykin, caused a lot of laughter and has remained in my memory:

So, brothers, I'm on guard duty at an artillery storehouse in the middle of a dark night. It's my first time. I'm standing and shivering. My eyes are goggling and I'm seeing a saboteur behind every bush. I got the fright of my life when I suddenly noticed a horse behind the barbed wire fence, walking about, snorting and grazing. Of course it had no idea it had entered the prohibited zone, where even a horse wasn't supposed to be, either by day or night.

And how could it have happened that, when I was making another turn around the storehouse, the same horse suddenly appeared inside the fence, alongside the storehouse? How had it managed to get inside the compound? What the devil had brought it here?

When I came across the horse my heart stopped and my hands trembled. I felt cold – obviously my hair was standing on end, lifting my cap, and an icy draught had blown under it. Now I saw life in a gloomy light: 'It's all up with me!' I murmured, 'it's probably not a horse but a walking charge of explosives, an equine Samurai! Now we'll all get blown up!'

I stood as if in a stupor. The horse stood too. What kind of fairy tale was this? Fear was fear, but service was still service – it was wartime after all. So I stepped closer on tiptoe. I got closer and closer – but the horse didn't move. Obviously it was well trained! And what if there was a charge with a timer fixed on it? I froze. No, no ticking was heard. I got closer to the storehouse to see things better. Aha, that's what it is! It turned out the horse had caught its halter on a stand. But maybe the enemy had tied the horse up to divert my attention? That thought threw me into a fever. I leaped away from that dumb beast, made myself ready, and calling up all my fortitude, set out to search the compound.

About three times I ran around, changing direction, looking where I needed to – and where I didn't. I checked everything suspicious. But what did I find? Nothing! I got so angry!

I returned to the horse. I see the brute is going to kick me.

'What next?' I think, 'it's gone completely mad!' I stopped and said to myself: 'You stop and think the situation over in cold blood. No rush. It's wartime but there's no room for haste.' And so I thought it over: maybe the horse has found itself here with no ulterior motive? What kind of consciousness does it have? Just reflexes! But isn't it a breach of Army regulations? I suppose so. But if, with its horse brains, it had managed to enter the zone without my being able to prevent it, that meant I was a duffer not a guard! And thinking logically, a sneaky saboteur could have already blown up the storehouse and me with it!

I avoided its dangerous hindquarters, and pressing myself against the stand, made for its head. 'Stand still, you noodle,' I whispered gently, 'what have you come to the storehouse for? It's dangerous here. You should understand that.' I pulled out the halter strap, which had obviously got caught when it was scratching its neck, and led it towards the exit.

Had she come out calmly all would have ended well. But no! It changed its mind near the exit. When I pulled harder it turned around, ready to strike, obviously intending to repay good with evil. Then the horse pulled the strap out of my hand and, sensing freedom, calmed down. I retreated to the safety of the storehouse. The horse snorted and set to grazing.

I felt uneasy again. What will my comrades say? What will my superiors say, when they find out about the incident in the night? The decision came straight away. I lay down on the grass, chose a moment when the horse turned its front to me, aimed and shot. A second shot went up in the air . . .

Next day, by special order from the top brass, I received a recommendation for . . . my vigilance.

One evening, after the roll-call, when it was dark and most of the prisoners had dispersed to their barracks, the roar of engines attracted everyone's attention: a convoy of trucks was slowly moving towards the gas chambers. Each vehicle was packed to the limit with people: men, women and children, holding onto each other. The lights of the first truck had barely disappeared into the Secret Grove when heartrending screams and wails reached our ears, attended by the barking of dogs and the shouts of SS men. The cries were heard so distinctly, one could discern individual voices, the weeping of women, the sobs of children. It was so unusual, so horrible and sinister, everyone froze to the spot. Then the dazzling glare of headlamps flared up from the direction of the gas chambers. A truck reversed past at high speed, its back raised: 'Dump trucks?' someone yelled. Trucks kept transporting people for about an hour, and the shouting and crying lasted almost till morning. Few people slept that horrible night. Even the prisoners, who were used to the horrors of the camp, were shaken to the core.

In the morning it became clear that many prisoners had lost their minds – there had been even more cases of suicide. There were so many dead bodies hanging in the ablution blocks that it was impossible to get through. There were no fewer in the blocks of the Jews, who'd recently arrived with the transports from Belgium and Holland. Despite the fact that transportation by truck to the gas chambers was not resumed after that night, the number of suicides and people losing their mind didn't abate.

Day and night huge pyres burned in the grove. Their crimson glow illuminated the camp at night, creating quaint, dancing shadows on the ground and walls. There was no escape from gloomy reflections, even in the darkest corners of the barracks, as these death-lights danced, poignantly affecting the prisoners' psyches. More and more frequently we'd wake up at night because of the wild ravings of those who'd lost their minds. They'd wander around in the dark, some looking for their children and kinfolk, trying to warn them about the mortal danger and save them from the gas chambers, the crematorium, the pyres. Those who accidentally approached the forbidden zone near the fence were shot by SS guards from the towers.

The number of suicides, especially during the hours of darkness, continued to grow like an epidemic. It reached such a scale that even the camp administration was startled. Of course, they didn't care about suicidal prisoners as such, but in their view, slaves who were physically fit had no right to take their own lives, as they were needed for work. Consequently an order was issued to form a so-called 'Night Crew' from Soviet POWs: its duty would be to prevent suicides. The crews consisted of small groups of two or three men. The number of suicides abruptly decreased after the very first watches by the Night Crew. The orderlies patrolled the camp and checked the ablution blocks and barracks. All suspects were taken under control. Sometimes the hopeless inmates were prevented from carrying out their intentions by persuasion – sometimes by force.

But the duties of the Soviet POWs resulted in a bold escape. Using their relative freedom during the night watches, several Russians and a Pole named Kovalenko, decided to escape. They got wire-cutters and dry planks. On a foggy night, hiding behind piles of earth thrown up along the fence during the excavation of ditches, they crawled up to the high-voltage wire and managed to cut the lower lines. The electrified wire rolled up after being cut, creating a gap, but it also sparked as it fused with the ground. The desperadoes rushed out of the camp and into the darkness – shapeless grey shadows shrouded by fog . . .

The silence of the night exploded with submachine-gun bursts and disjointed shouts. Sporadic fire from the guards on the southern and northern sides of the camp joined the submachine-guns of the western side. Prisoners awakened by the shooting pressed themselves into their bunks – the most experienced spread out on the floor. Few dared to look outside and even fewer ran out of the barracks. The fog hid everything like a smoke screen. No one knew about the escape – and those few who did remained silent. And so all was confusion: 'What's happened, why are they shooting?' Then the siren began to howl: 'Escape! Escape!' Orderlies from the Night Crew were returning to the barracks – the shooting had caught them unawares, and since it was impossible in the fog to work out what had happened, they decided to join their comrades. The escape happened two hours before dawn. SS men and dogs were thrown in pursuit of the escapees.

Dawn had barely broken when sharp whistles announced a roll-call. Embittered Blockführers were flying about the camp yelling and cursing. They were desperate to know who'd escaped and how many – as indeed we all were. The word 'Schnell, schnell!' ('Quick, quick!') was being conveyed along a human chain from the very mouth of the Lagerführer. Suddenly it rippled through the rows of Soviet POWs: Mishka Zmey's not here, nor is Vas'ka Golovokrut. There was a minute's bewilderment, then everyone began to talk, discussing the escape. 'Ruhe! Achtung! Mützen ab!' bawled a paled Blockältester, who'd already been advised that two men were not present – either in the line-up or in the barracks. The Blockführer twice counted up the men, examined the empty barracks, then ran to report to the Lagerführer.

They kept us standing in line for several hours. This was a way of intimidating the prisoners, as if to say: 'It's your own fault for breaching the regulations!' By now everyone in the camp knew that Mishka Zmey and Vas'ka Golovokrut ('Zmey' and 'Golovokrut' were nicknames – Mishka's real surname was Porozov, and he was from the City of Kourgan) had escaped together with the Pole, Kovalenko, who knew the countryside around Auschwitz.

In the middle of the day news arrived that the escapees had been captured. The SS men dropped three naked, disfigured corpses near the entrance checkpoint. But why was there no damage to the bodies, just disfiguring of the faces? No, the escapees hadn't been found: these were certainly not they. Later, 'Chaps' told us in secret that dogs had led the SS men to a train station, where the trail went cold. They wouldn't move any further because there were no more footprints.

The Night Crew was disbanded the same day. A Blockältester lined up all the Soviet POWs and conveyed the Lagerführer's order: 'If the Russians abuse the confidence placed in them and try to escape again, twenty men will be shot for each of the escapees.'

But the escape of our comrades had a huge influence on the prisoners' morale – especially ours. No, the Fascist butchers were not almighty! And no threats could root out the dream of escape from our minds: the dream so successfully made reality by the bold courage of our comrades. Thus the impetus to escape remained strong. Every one of us nurtured this hope in his soul. It gave us strength to endure all suffering, maintaining courage and faith in the future. Escape was a dream, and each of us had accomplished it more than a dozen times in our minds. But the high-voltage wire remained a most serious obstacle, looming large in our imaginations. Everyone knew it would be impossible to get through alone. An organized force was needed. Only cohesion and force could overcome any hurdle. The escape of lone persons – even the most resolute – was a matter of luck. And how long would we have to wait for it?

Thus, in conversations and arguments, the idea of a joint escape was being conceived and strengthened. Sergei (sadly my memory failed to retain his surname – it may have been Vinogradov) stirred up this idea. Sergei was of medium height, a bit round-shouldered. Frostbitten feet made him stoop even more. An oblong face, high forehead dissected by wrinkles, mouth drawn into a contemptuous grimace – at first sight he created an unfavourable impression. But closer contact revealed a remark-able personality with strong self-control. Speaking with a passionate confidence, it was Sergei who initiated that un-forgettable night-meeting, destined to play such a decisive role in the fate of Soviet POWs at Birkenau.

Late August, evening. The moon was not up yet. The calm air – saturated with moisture from the surrounding marshes and tinged with sweetish smoke from smouldering pyres – was beginning to cool off. The tiny lights of 'roll-your-owns' glowed bright against the dark outline of the barracks. Having overcome fatigue, and at the expense of their leisure time, prisoners were talking about the past, present and future.

As if by accident, several Soviet POWs gathered in the lonesome spot between the barracks, hidden by shadows. Here were Sergei, Andrei Zaitsev, Vasili Dotsenko, Petr Mishin, Nikolai Vasiliev, Pavel Sten'kin and I. 'Alright,' said Sergei, 'we can start. Comrades, after much hesitation and long discussions with my friend Andrei Zaitsev, we chose you to discuss the issue of a joint escape. The issue is very serious. We've seen each other many times, and many times we've spoken about it. We're here because our thoughts agree. Is it worth uniting our efforts in organizing this escape? Speak openly.'

'What's there to talk about? We all agree! Keep going.'

'We trust all of you and we're glad we haven't made a mistake in our choice. Right, Andrei? We ain't gonna get out of here alive to tell about what's been happening. We'll be wiped out. Now the Fascists are triumphant: they're on the Volga, they've surrounded Leningrad, occupied the Ukraine and Belorussia. They trumpet out that Moscow has been taken as well. Lies! The French who arrived yesterday deny it categorically and say that Moscow is not Paris and the Fascists will get their neck broken over there. They're right! We know the history of our Motherland and we're sure the Russians will win. How can we help achieve this victory? By our spirit and self-control! The individual attempts to escape should cease for now. Under current conditions they can't be successful. Only a mass escape will do: one that will show these murderers it's not easy to beat the Soviet people; that the Russians have remained Russians even in the death camp; that their spirit hasn't been broken. Am I right?'

'Right, Sergei! Dead right! What's required from us?'

'Practical proposals are needed. For example, what should be done to support the will to escape? And what should be done to prevent individual escape attempts until a unified plan is worked out? I suggest we form an escape committee of seven or eight men. Each member of the committee should recruit a group or "cell" of twelve men around himself, convince them that there's a real plan of escape, and make preparations.'

'Who else can be recruited onto the committee without risk?'

'Let's not be in a hurry. It needs thinking over.'

'Right, I'll summarize: we resolve to form a committee to prepare a mass escape. From tomorrow, each member of the head-quarters committee will pick a dozen men for preparation, of whom he'll be responsible. Also, each member will have to prepare escape proposals for discussion. This is the most difficult question, on which the success of the whole business will depend. The main condition for a proposal is that it must feature a joint escape, in which all those who wish will be able to take part, regardless of nationality. The consequences of the escape will have to be considered too. Should it succeed, it will be a joy that will raise morale and faith, give strength to thousands of people . . .'

'I move that Sergei be put in charge of the escape!'

'No objections.'

Next day I saw a completely different man in the bent and limping Sergei. How wrong the impression of a man based on his looks can be! One evening Sergei and I met to clarify some issue that had arisen. So as not to draw attention, we headed towards the ablution block. Sergei was walking, breathing heavily and shifting his frostbitten feet with great effort. I was looking at the road, rammed with crushed stone, and at those shuffling feet: horrible pictures of the recent past were rising in my memory, causing a shudder . . .

Winter. Thousands of half-clothed prisoners are digging drains on a huge snow-covered bog, lashed by a biting wind. Hands stiff with cold, the handles of wheel-barrows are tied to wrists; shovels are wielded with difficulty. Back-breaking work under the furious shouts of Kapos armed with sticks and whips. The moans of those being beaten. Exhausted prisoners lay on the ground among the corpses. Only by constant movement can one stay alive. It's especially hard on the feet. Wooden clogs are best – they give some warmth and it's possible to wrap rags around the feet. They don't sink in swampy ground, but icy water seeps in . . .

And so it was day after day. No one knows how many lives were taken by the winter and spring, how much blood and how many tears the water of the bog had borne away. Every square metre of Birkenau represented dozens of dead bodies: victims whose lives had snapped under terrible suffering and torment. Few had survived that horrible time. I looked again at Sergei and couldn't help but ask: 'Sergei, how are you going to escape with feet like that?' He grinned and sighed: 'I don't yet know myself!

I'll do my best to substitute them with my head . . .'

That was Sergei. His friend, Andrei Zaitsev, was the exact opposite. Tall, well-proportioned and neat – even in the camp conditions – with an open, handsome face and a big bald patch framed by a silvery strip of hair: he inspired confidence at first sight. There were rumours Zaitsev had been a regular Soviet officer but he always maintained he'd been a chef in a Moscow restaurant! Zaitsev was cautious and never acted rashly. We surmised that the friendship between Sergei and Zaitsev had begun before their time in the camp, for they had common acquaintances and friends.

I'll never forget the other members of the escape or 'head-quarters' committee: Vasili Dotsenko was another tall and handsome man. He possessed the iron patience of a father and the tender heart of a mother. He couldn't look with indifference on youths and children in the camp, and always tried to support them with an affectionate word, in order to cheer them up. Despite heavy bouts of radiculitis (inflammation of the spinal nerves) Vasya [a diminutive of Vasili – trans.] held up well. Petr Mishin, a quiet, inconspicuous student, worked in the camp laundry with Dotsenko. Everyone called him 'Pet'ka from AU'. He'd spent several months in the Auschwitz bunker, where the Gestapo sent all political suspects. Nikolai Vasiliev, a Muscovite, worked in the hospital. Many Russians – and not only Russians – had found assistance from this kind-hearted medical orderly. A tablet, a patch of bandage, some advice, had the most curative properties. Kolya [a diminutive of Nikolai – trans.] had put dressings on my wound several times. Pavel Sten'kin, a Mordvin [a small nation in European Russia – trans.] by nationality, was from Perm. He'd been a frontier guard and experienced the first morning of the war while on watch. He limped badly, as a shell splinter embedded in his leg had decided to come out. A Polish doctor dug out this piece of metal while Pavlik [a diminutive of Pavel – trans.] was held tightly by the arms and legs. Pavlik was the only survivor from the group that excavated the tunnel under the barbed-wire fence of camp 308 in the Żagań forest.

The escape committee knew about my friendship with Heniek, the Polish electrician: so I was charged with finding out from him whether or not it would be possible to turn off the voltage at the right moment. A frank discussion took place in front of his buddy, also a Pole. Answering my silent question, expressed with a look, Heniek smiled and said this guy could be trusted even more than he. Nevertheless, I concealed the existence of the escape committee, saying I alone had a proposition to make. Heniek listened attentively. We discussed all the options for switching off the voltage. But Heniek said that after Kovalenko's escape the alarm system had been upgraded: now it would be enough for one cable to touch a concrete post, or the ground, and a siren would switch on automatically.

The results of the discussion were less than favourable: although Heniek agreed to switch off the high voltage – and also the power to the lighting system – it was clear his life would be endangered as a result. As it would be impossible to save him, this option was abandoned.

Heniek's comrade then made an offer: he would try to break the barbed wire between two concrete posts by felling a wooden lamp-post onto it. He even showed us a suitable place: there, on the southern side of the camp, was just such a lamp-post – almost directly in front of a watch tower. If it were felled towards the fence it would fall exactly on the wire. The proximity of the watch tower was all to the good: it would be possible to overwhelm the guard with a hail of rocks and overturn it. In this case shooting from neighbouring towers would be quite harmless in the dark. And so we stuck with this idea. But in order to check the viability of the plan, one of the construction crews was charged with the task of 'dropping' one such lamp-post on a wire fence, for which the voltage had not yet been turned on. Of course it would have to be done very skilfully, so as to make the fall seem accidental. How much work, ingenuity and resourcefulness it cost to perform this experiment! The key thing was to avoid any suspicion that the act was deliberate. But when the post eventually fell we were bitterly disappointed. In falling, it only tore a few of the upper wires stretched between the concrete posts, leaving the rest intact. There was no more hope. We had to look for other options.

Days and weeks flew by, but escape plans were at a standstill and tension was growing. Members of the escape committee warned that their groups or 'cells' were demanding action. At the same time, several events occurred to electrify the prisoners even more.

The SK – a penal squad consisting of Poles – mutinied, having been driven to despair by torment and brutality. Usually, those for whom immediate retribution had been commuted to physical and emotional torture would be sent to this crew. The SS guards tormented the penalized men with especial brutality. Death was frequently more desirable than life for these prisoners, but the Fascist sadists would delay it intentionally, enjoying the suffering of their victims. The latter were forced do difficult – yet completely pointless – tasks, like moving heavy rocks from one spot to another, or digging trenches and then backfilling them straight away.

On the day of the mutiny, the SK prisoners were collecting rocks, tree branches and rubbish outside the camp, on its western side. It was strictly prohibited to straighten up during this kind of work. An SS-Mann armed with a stick walked between the bent prisoners. At the edge of the meadow stood two guards with submachine-guns. Several Poles, exhausted by the heat and un-natural posture, fell over and were brutally beaten, being unable to get up again. Another man wavered, almost dropping, but held on and managed to stand upright. At that moment he was assailed by a hail of blows from the stick. He collapsed, covered with blood. But all of a sudden something happened that the Fascists – used to implicit obedience – never expected. The prisoners fell upon their tormentors, immediately killing the stick-wielding SS-Mann and one of the submachine-gunners. The other guard, having gathered his wits, rushed away. The prisoners who survived, instead of making use of the submachine-gun, ran around in all directions. The remaining SS-Mann opened fire, aided by guards on the watch towers.

The consequences were tragic. The SS selected 200 Poles during evening roll-call, tied their hands with wire and drove them to the gas chambers, guarded by dogs. All the Poles were burned. In the morning, prisoners from the Sonderkommando said the Poles had died with pride and dignity. They calmly entered the gas chamber singing their national anthem. Even the SS guards were astounded by their fortitude.

Several days later another tragic event took place. Kapo Number One secretly told me about an overheard conversation between Sonderführers: notification had arrived that several hundred POWs – Soviet officers – had been sent to Auschwitz for immediate extermination. They'd arrive in a day or two under heavy guard. I immediately relayed the news to my comrades from the committee. They decided to warn our countrymen about the impending danger at any cost. But how to do it? No one knew when they'd arrive at Birkenau. The committee charged reliable comrades with the task of keeping their eyes on the road, along which prisoners had been commonly transported to the gas chambers. Vasili Dotsenko took a piece of white pasteboard and drew in large letters: 'YOU'LL BE GASSED IN THE BATH-HOUSE'. No more words would fit on it! The pasteboard was fixed under someone's blouse, so as to show it to the comrades passing by. But all this preparation turned out to be futile. The POW officers were transported in the middle of the night under a reinforced escort. There was no chance to warn them. All were exterminated the very same night.

A poem by our comrade Alexandrovich contributed greatly to the fighting spirit of the Soviet POWs. Despite its contents – full of anguish, pain and sadness – it inspired a zeal to break out of this hell; to break out so as to tell of the inhuman suffering inflicted on countless people:

The brutal monster of the brown plague,
Conceived by a fanatic in sickly raving,
Born of vandals and lords of darkness,
By the will of spiteful fate, appeared like an ulcer

In the town of Auschwitz.
And Auschwitz became a town of murderers,
A town of bloody villainy,
A grave it has become: Osventsim-Auschwitz,
A symbol of inhuman suffering.
People are killed and tortured here in thousands
By bayonets and sticks, by whip and flying lead.
They're starved to death, stifled with gas
By murderers led by a lunatic rogue.
Day and night the sparkling pyres and sinister crematorium
Burn and glow,
Turning people, love, hopes and dreams
Into gas, smoke and ashes.
But the time will come when the twinkling stars,
The bushes, trees and smoky leaves,
The Earth soaked with blood and tears,
The bright Sun and pallid Moon,
Will tell everything about these horrible days.
They'll tell how mothers foreseeing misfortune
Looked at their small children
With eyes mad from horror,
While they played joyfully
In the gas chamber.
They'll tell how heroes died
As victims of tyranny, believing in God,
Hands stretched out to him in entreaty
As SS Sonderführers threw babies alive
Into the raging, seething fire;
And as they laughing drove mothers
With dog, whip and stick,
As they brutally beat the stubborn
With their heavy 'Gott mit uns' buckles,
They'll tell the nightmarish true story
Of the hard times, sorrowful and gloomy,
That befell tens of thousands, young and old,
Who awaited their tragic lot

In Birkenau's storehouse of living corpses.
They'll tell about us as well,
About the first prisoners of the accursed swamp,
About those on whom the death gas was tested;
Who used to live next to the black death,
Who served as an example for the deprived
By their fortitude and firmness.
They'll tell about the hidden desire
Of those who didn't want to die that senseless death,
The desire that was vast and inspiring,
Giving strength to defeat despair.
They'll tell how we used to dream of freedom,
Of life, of happiness, of former joy,
Dreamed of struggle fierce and holy,
Of our beloved homeland, dear as Mother.

A proposal to escape during 'search duty' was put to the committee. Search duty was frequently performed, as that summer there had been an unusual number of escape attempts. Needless to say, the role of those involved in search work was more than unseemly. After all, any hidden prisoner awaiting a chance to escape would be immediately handed over to the administration – and the fate of such desperadoes was well known to everyone. But the more this proposal was discussed the more attractive it seemed. Apart from the fact that the Poles – on whose assistance we were counting – wouldn't have a chance to take part, all other conditions were such that no better chance to break out could be found in our situation. The decision of the committee was unanimous: to organize an escape while on search duty – it was the only opportunity for a large group of people to get outside the camp.

But Soviet POWs had never been selected for search duty! Thus, all members of the committee were charged with the following task: to spread by any means the notion that the Russians were keen to take part in search duties; that the Russians, instead of standing in line and waiting until someone found an offender, were eager to find him themselves and release both administration and guards from the torment of long, tedious roll-calls. We were firmly convinced this sham desire of the Soviet POWs would be reported to the camp administration by their spies and boot-lickers. We easily convinced the Blockältester of our sincerity and he duly made the Blockführer aware of it. We even inveigled 'Chaps' into the ruse, though it pricked our conscience. But our calculations proved correct. Some ten days later we heard the long-awaited order: 'Russians, out for line-up!'

Most Soviet POWs rushed to the centre of the Appellplatz with joy: reason being that it was debilitating to stand in line for an hour or two – even more so after a day of tiring work – so it was much easier to be on the move. That was why our crew had found such fervent support, for our *real* intentions were known only to committee members. Of course, the SS men and Kapos found their own explanations for it.

We displayed such an ostentatious energy during the search that our Blockältester earned a commendation, which he immediately announced, hoping to inspire even greater efforts. Indeed, the Russians searched with a hue-and-cry: crawling into pipes, cellars, ditches and trenches; and into all possible holes, where even the Kapos didn't dare creep. This outburst of energy was taken for compliance and eagerness: but in reality, those who'd been initiated into the escape preparations – and those who new nothing but had a secret desire to escape – were using the search for reconnaissance. All the time they were examining and calculating. Meanwhile, not a little effort had to be applied to prevent an unauthorized attempt, which would frustrate all our careful preparations.

During search duty the location of our proposed breakout was pinpointed. It was as if someone had deliberately prepared it! For in the north-west corner of the fence there was a 20-metre gap in the wire. The men of the Sonderkommando were driven through this gap to work, while building materials were sent through to a construction site, where foundations for a crematorium and gas chamber had been laid. In front of the gap, some 10–15 metres away from the fence, was a watch tower containing an SS guard. And beyond that was a small, sparse wood.

At last, when everyone had got used to the Russians being sent out for search duty, and these missions had begun to be considered mandatory, the committee set a date for the escape. It was to be 6 November and wasn't subject to change. In order to make sure the attempt went ahead on schedule, one of the crews working in the camp under construction was charged with the task of faking an individual escape attempt on that day: this would guarantee search duty took place. The plan called for the body of a dead prisoner to be secretly buried in an appropriate spot: but not a Russian, so as not to get the Russians taken off search duty.

For the days remaining till the escape date, the committee members ordered their 'cells' – each one consisting of a dozen escapees – to remain alert, and to prepare for the breakout by gathering clothes and disguising camp numbers on their chests with tattoos.

It's impossible to convey the state of the prisoners during those days, their feverish excitement. Some were wavering, fearful of taking chances. Others were openly against the plan. Time and again arguments would erupt spontaneously, going as far as direct accusations of cowardice and insults. The opponents of the escape asserted that the situation, conditions, and time of year were unfavourable for escape; that the escape would bring no good to anyone; that there was no need for it. Indeed, the situation and the time of the year were against us, but the vast majority of comrades were in favour of the venture. And in fact, the madness of this desire, the madness of escape – bold and courageous – was quite justified. We felt the hot breath of the defenders of Moscow – behind the concrete walls and barbed wire. Escape was the only contribution we could make to the common struggle for liberation; to the destruction of bloodthirsty Fascism. It was impossible not to consider this patriotic impulse, not to take it into account.

One can only admire the fortitude of the Birkenau prisoners – people physically weak but strong in spirit; people who well understood that to run away in November, just before the cold frosts, when Nature became an accomplice of the deadly foe instead of an ally, required a great deal of will power. But the climate really was the least of our worries: within minutes of escape sirens would broadcast the news far and wide; hundreds of SS guards, aided by packs of trained dogs, would then give chase; while we'd be running without knowledge of the language and locality; and through territory populated by people for whom catching escapees was not just a moral pleasure but also a chance to gain material benefits. And yet – like soldiers in a bayonet charge – we didn't think about death. People with no Motherland, people without a care for country and kinfolk, could not have taken such a step . . .

Sixth of November 1942. Tomorrow would be a significant day – the 25th Anniversary of the Great October Revolution [i.e. according to the old Julian calendar used in pre-Revolutionary Russia – trans.]. This date added special enthusiasm and resolve to all our actions. Driven by a patriotic tradition, we were eager to present our Motherland a gift; to celebrate the date dear to the Soviet people with the impulse of our hearts. By this gift to our Motherland we wanted to show the Fascist sadists that neither torture nor outright physical extermination had broken the morale of the Soviet people; that even in this hell they hadn't forgotten their Motherland, and in all their thoughts were back there, where bloody battles for freedom and independence were being fought.

Today it was exactly thirteen months since the first transport with Soviet POWs had arrived at Auschwitz. Thirteen terrible months! At midday the signal – a rag attached to a high pole – was given from a pre-arranged spot in the camp under construction: everyone get ready – a corpse has been hidden! Those who hadn't managed to prepare were in a hurry. They shaved, tried to spruce up their clothes, or endured the final needle-pricks of ink that covered the camp numbers on their chests with plain pictures. Everyone's been warned, everyone knows. Feverish excitement. It's easy to distinguish those who've chosen to stay: for even though the decision lurks in the darkest corner of their souls, it's revealed by furtive glances from restless eyes. It's impossible for everyone to make the breakout. Many are sick or so emaciated that escape is out of question. Of course, there are some who have showed faintheartedness at the last moment.

How slowly the time drags! It's a sunny day. Many are loudly rejoicing: there will be a thick ground mist tonight. Meanwhile, in the sky, the Great Bear will be our guide.

Right on cue, the command to line up for search duty was given after evening roll-call. We lined up in more disorder than ever before. Everyone was rushing to take position in the rows, which were supposed to consist of five men each: consequently a hurly-burly erupted. It appeared that more than eighty men had stepped forward for the line-up and the latecomers – knowing that only neatly aligned groups of ten would be allowed to march out – were trying to sneak into the fifteenth and the sixteenth rows. There was no chance of sneaking further forward, for the SS guards were already counting people from both sides of the column. Eventually the hubbub ended when an SS-Mann, yelling furiously, counted off seventy men, separating this column from the rest. More than fifteen men – Petr Mishin and Nikolai Vasiliev among them – stood on the road, helplessly watching their comrades walk away. Some waved their hands to us. My heart shrank with pain. I wanted to shout: 'Farewell, comrades!'

The Russians, coming out into the territory of the camp under construction, immediately scattered for the search. Playing for time, we slowly moved toward the agreed assembly point. We examined everything on the way, turning over boards and scattering piles of planks. Our pockets were full of 'weapons' – a variety of heavy objects. Our spirits were high but anxiety showed in all our words and actions. Strained jokes and nervous laughter were heard all around. Some were even trying to sing.

At last the sun slid behind the horizon and we gathered near the gap in the fence. A guard calmly looked down at us from the watch tower. Away to our left, pyres were blazing deep in the Secret Grove. Further beyond, the crematorium was puffing out black smoke. All was quiet. Suddenly something completely unforeseen happened. At the very last moment – just as the signal was about to be given – we heard the snarling of a dog accompanied by swearing in German. This was immediately followed by the appearance of the Sonderkommando, heading towards us out of the grove behind the watch tower almost at a run. Next moment, when the men of the Sonderkommando were already on our side of the tower, we heard cursing and yelling, a shot, and again the German Shepherd dog's snarl, turning into a squeal. Urged by SS guards the Sonderkommando men ran past us. Two Sonderführers – pistols in hand – flanked the column, while one brought up the rear with a dog. Having noticed our Blockältester, one of the running Sonderführers shouted to him to pick up a corpse and carry it to the camp. The Blockältester immediately selected four men, and raising his voice so the guard on the tower could hear, ordered loudly: 'Go and pick up the corpse!' I found myself in this quartet. We were almost under the watch tower. The SS guard was quietly watching us as before. Beyond the tower freedom beckoned.

We picked up the murdered man. I glanced towards my comrades. Hundreds of eyes were fixed on us. Strained postures. Nervous expectation on faces. Dozens of prisoners froze like a spring pressed to the limit. It was a volcano before eruption, wherein everything was burning, boiling, seething. Suddenly a voice cut through the silence: 'For the Motherland! Forward!' A discordant 'Hurrah!' exploded, unleashing a hail of rocks, lumps of iron and assorted missiles at the SS watchman. Then, like a raging avalanche, the prisoners surged forward, toppling the tower and scattering into the forest through the created gap.

The swiftness of our rush, and the speed with which we crossed the deadly strip between the fence and the trees, meant we penetrated the forest without loss, as submachine-guns rattled behind. We tried to run in silence, though it seemed that branches and brushwood were breaking under our feet with deafening cracks. I heard Sergei's voice for the last time, some distance behind: 'Don't rush! Don't waste your strength. Run sensibly!'

Neither his face nor the faces of other comrades were visible in the dark forest. Then the siren began to howl, drowning everything out. The pursuit had begun.

The darkness was growing thicker and thicker. Shadows flickered among the trees. No voices were heard off. There was no point looking or calling for our lost comrades. Faster, faster, forward . . .

There's a whole group of us running. We stick together. The presence of comrades sustains strength and courage. Suddenly the forest disappears. There's a river in front of us. Without hesitation we roll down the sloping bank to the water. Fortunately it's no more than a metre and a half deep, although the current is strong. The river is about 20 metres wide. Soaked clothes hamper movement. My body, warmed by running and nervous strain, doesn't feel the water's icy chill. At last we reach the far bank, completely overgrown by low bushes. We scramble out of the water, helping each other. There are eight of us . . .

Hurriedly shaking off the water we rushed into a hollow, obscured by a shroud of thick fog. We rejoiced at this, as if it were a forest. Above us the Great Bear – our only guide – could be discerned through the mist, as if through a lace curtain. We walked quickly, not letting each other out of sight. The fog grew seemingly thinner. Suddenly a dog barked somewhere ahead. Judging from its tone it wasn't a German Shepherd, just a mongrel. Was there really a village in front of us? If so, they already knew about the escape. We stopped to discuss the situation. This minute's delay proved fatal.

Somewhere on our right we heard the noise of approaching engines. Then, about 40 metres to our front – the direction from where the dog had barked – a vehicle drove from right to left. Against the backdrop of the sky we could see it was an open truck full of troops. Another followed, making short stops to let SS soldiers jump off. The thought scorched me: we're surrounded! That bloody dog! If only it hadn't barked we'd have made it across the road. A brief exchange of whispers followed. We decided to split into two groups of four and sneak towards the road, in order to break out. The first group set off straight ahead. I crawled to the right with my group.

After covering some 40 or 50 metres we came across a shallow swamp with a fairly solid bed. Again, a vehicle appeared on our right. As it moved, flares began soaring from it, separated by short intervals. The first salvo took us by surprise. We had to submerge into the swamp with the slime almost over our heads. We plucked some bundles of wiry grass. When a flare went up, illuminating everything around, we'd freeze – our eyes poking out of the water, the tops of our heads hidden under the grassy bundles. In this way at least we could look around: the high road skirted the swamp in a broad semi-circle; SS men stood on it 100 metres apart. We continued crawling towards the road during the intervals between the flares. Finally the swamp came to an end.

A gentle rise. The vehicle with flares was now somewhere far to the left. We were crawling, slowly pressing ourselves against the ground. Someone made a false step: we heard some yelling ahead of us and two shots shattered the silence – whew whew – the bullets whizzed over our heads. By instinct I threw myself sideways, then froze. All quiet. I looked around: no one was near. I quickly crawled back – no one in sight. I began whispering signals. No one responded. And at that moment I felt the first fear. Yes, the most real fear – fear of solitude. Was I really on my own now? I tried to take myself in hand. Having calmed myself down I resumed searching and almost crashed into Viktor Kouznetsov, who was in the same situation. No time for rejoicing. Now we began looking for the others. Nothing. Two of our guys – both named Pavlik – had disappeared in the fog.

We decided to edge right, away from the fire of the jumpy SS-Mann. Suddenly we came upon a ditch: no doubt water was draining into the bog from the opposite side of the road embankment. Given the water was draining, there had to be a channel for it through the embankment. We crawled towards the high road full of hope. The fog was getting thinner and thinner and the SS men showed clearly against the background of the sky. One stood about 40 metres from us, another about 60 metres. Holding submachine-guns against their waists they were looking towards the swamp. We approached the embankment, but instead of a channel found a narrow pipe, into which only a head might have squeezed. What could we do? Below us the swamp was still shrouded in mist, but the high road above was clear. Pressing ourselves into the very ground, huddling close to each other, our thoughts raced – looking for a way out. Fortunately our wet, filthy clothes offered some camouflage: but the headlamps of the first passing vehicle would reveal our position.

We discussed the situation in whispers, all the time straining to catch every sound. From behind the swamp – the direction from which we'd come – we heard shots, shouts and colourful Russian swearing. Viktor pushed me and nodded at the road. The vehicle from which the flares were launched was already on its way back. The flares were illuminating first one side, then the other, at short intervals of two or three minutes. We heard the dull click of a signal pistol and followed the flash with our eyes. What to do? In a couple of minutes the vehicle would be upon us and must surely catch us in its lights. Our only chance was to dash forward and try to break through during the intervals between flares. I turned to Viktor, almost invisible in the profound darkness: 'Viten'ka my friend, look at me. Look! Can you see me? Tell me, can you see me?' – 'No. No, I can't.' Another flare soared, sparked and died. 'Right, now once again . . . The same? Good. Take off your boots and stick them in your blouse. Check your pockets. There mustn't be a sound . . .'

A burst of disorderly shooting followed by curses and shouts. The clear moan of a seriously wounded man. That was one of our comrades. The vehicle was coming closer and closer, its head-lamps striking sideways from the high road. An additional searchlight was now clearly visible aboard the vehicle, momen-tarily illuminating a dark haycock with shadows flashing by.

The Fascists' plan was clear: to keep us all surrounded till morning. A furious anger seethed in my soul. We were ready. Once again, goggling our eyes, we looked at each other. No more doubts. Pitch darkness remained for several seconds. It was quite enough for a spurt across the road. There was about half a kilometre to the vehicle. We made ourselves ready as the searchlight switched to the opposite side from us. The next flare fizzled out with a barely audible crackle and we darted across the road like cats. Then we held our breath, slid down the slope, and froze. Heartbeats hammered at my temples as another flare soared . . .

How slowly time was dragging. Faster! Faster! It's gone out! We crawled away from the road on our bellies. The dark silhouette of some building showed up ahead. Here we were in front of it, then past it. We looked back. As before, the SS men were standing in tense postures – but now with their backs to us. Yes, their backs to us! Suddenly, vehicle lights illuminated the abandoned, half-ruined shack. We worked our way round to the shadowed side and leant against the wall, exhausted and trembling. The vehicle sped past, plunging the shack into darkness. Our plan had worked.

Unable to hold back the sobs, Viktor and I hugged each other. After this burst of joy we discussed our next move. We decided to head west towards Germany, to put our pursuers off the scent, before striking south to Czechoslovakia. On this night we needed to break away as far as possible from this accursed spot. Having glanced once more at the cordon to wish our comrades good luck, we set off.

Early on the morning of 7 November we reached the edge of a young grove. It started raining but we didn't mind. On the contrary we were glad: after all, it was washing our footprints away – the dogs were no longer a danger.

The human body is an astounding thing. Under normal circumstances dozens of diseases would have attacked us that night, and the efforts of many people would have been required to save us from death. But how were we doing? We were fine! Striding cheerfully, choosing firmer ground. And yet we were badly tired. We knew that if we stopped to sit down there'd be no strength to stand up again. Only will power kept us moving. The desire to live was winning over fatigue. In our minds we were already in our Motherland. By now this remarkable day had already been celebrated in the East; was still being celebrated in Siberia; and was just about to be celebrated in Moscow. Meanwhile, fighting continued. And here, we had our own personal battlefront.

We looked around as we walked – were there any signs of dwellings nearby? I helped Viktor climb a tree: a young forest spread around us. We decided to spend our first night of freedom at its very heart.

Suddenly, in a small glade, we saw a light awning filled with hay, lying on a low dais. Obviously it was forage stocked for the winter. Looked like it'd been stocked long ago, for the hay was darkly discoloured. We quickly took off our clothes and wrung them out. Viktor crawled under the awning with my assistance and made a lair in the hay. Disguising the traces, I followed him. We lay down in rare bliss. A moment later we fell into oblivion.

In the evening – rested, warmed up and heartened – we set out again on our long trek. We journeyed west one more night, then turned south towards the Czechoslovakian border. There, up in the Tatra mountains, Partisans were hiding. Now we marched without noticing fatigue because we were striding towards life. Long live freedom! Long live life!

CHAPTER TEN

Interrogation

Andrei Pogozhev and his comrade, Viktor Kouznetsov, walked for a full day before stowing away on a train heading east. Arrested at one of the stops and taken to the local police station, the two fugitives were separated. They never saw each other again.

For Andrei, a period of intense interrogation followed, eventually leading to incarceration in another camp, which by his own testimony, 'wasn't much different from [. . .] Auschwitz – the same roll-calls, starvation, torments by the guards'. Ten days later he was transferred to a small labour camp he calls 'Khvudobrek'.

On 9 May 1943 Andrei, accompanied by three other POWs, slipped out of the camp under cover of darkness, heading east towards the Carpathians. Eventually arriving at the Polish–Ukrainian border, the fugitives were scattered by shots from a German patrol. Andrei, now alone, continued his journey east with false papers provided by his erstwhile companions, giving his name as 'Mikhail Ivanovich Khomenko'. Hoping to find a Partisan detachment, he crossed the Western Ukraine aided by villagers terrorized by Germans and a 'Polizei' of collaborationists known as the 'Kushcha'.

Thus, as he approached the Poltavshina District, Andrei was in high spirits, singing 'as if I were striding on a free land'. But his joy was premature. Having been offered hospitality at a villager's house, Andrei was betrayed by the hostess and arrested by the

Fascist 'Kushcha' men. Taking him for a Partisan, the Polizei locked Andrei in a small room with a boarded window while they discussed his fate:

> I listened to the Polizei talking in the corridor. One of them said: 'Let the kid go or they'll hang him. A pity, he's still young.' Another replied: 'What if the Partisans catch you? Will they let you go?' But a third stood up for me: 'Of course, if you get caught they won't pardon you, but your brother has been recently deported to Germany. What if he escapes? Good luck to him on his way back home, because guys like us may catch him and hang him. And what then?' Having talked for another couple of minutes they left. It became quiet and grew dark outside, and only the guard's steps were heard . . .

Painstakingly tearing the plywood board off the window, Andrei eventually made his escape, dropping into a yard and bolting into the darkness, leaving the 'Kushcha' men to their drinking songs.

In the Mirgorodski District, with the front line drawing near, Andrei found work on a state-owned farm or 'sovkhoz': 'We uprooted stumps in the daytime. In the evenings we listened to the approaching artillery cannonade.' Desperate to rejoin the Army, Andrei set off again, encountering retreating German units along the way, obliging him to return to the safety of the sovkhoz. But with the German Army implementing a scorched earth policy prior to evacuation, Andrei was forced to move yet again: to a smaller farm, further from the high road. There, while labouring in a watermelon patch, Andrei heard the news: 'an old watchman, crying for joy, told us that the Red Army had arrived at the sovkhoz.'

Immediately returning to the sovkhoz, Andrei found the commanding Soviet officer, announced his true identity, and was sent to join a mortar company. By evening, he was heading back west as a Red Army soldier. But a week later, Andrei – as an ex-

POW – fell under the scrutiny of the regimental osobi otdel or 'security unit' and was sent to a 'training regiment' at Mirgorod to be debriefed. To his disappointment, Andrei saw no further active service.

Finally, in 1965, Fate added a twist to Andrei's tale, pulling him back to Germany as a prosecution witness in a war crimes trial. There, in a courtroom in Frankfurt-am-Main, Andrei Alexandrovich Pogozhev, ex-Auschwitz prisoner No. 1418, confronted his captors one last time . . .

For many years I'd been trying to forget the most horrible things. I'd been trying to preserve only good and dear recollections from that terrible time. I thought I'd managed it, but it was just a sincere self-delusion. A part of my life had been hidden in the most secret storeroom of my memory: now the doors had opened and the nightmarish past was bearing down on me. Did I imagine that one day I'd have to remember and relive the tragedy of my days in Hell? Did I imagine that I'd be reunited, face to face, with the butchers whose torments had left their marks on my body – marks I still carried? Of course not! But I had to remember . . .

During testimonies I didn't look at the SS men sitting in the dock: the feeling of contempt and blind hatred for them, which had lived in me since that very time and which had become more acute with the recollections and the atmosphere of the trial, prevented me. I didn't want to look at them, and in fact, turned away from them in a pointed manner. It would have been unbearably painful to see their faces again, and relive the experience of my own weakness and vulnerability. For now, just as before, it would be impossible to physically avenge the tortures, humiliations and insults I and my comrades endured. Thus, the best I could do was display my complete indifference towards them. I told myself they didn't exist any more, despite the fact they were alive and standing before me; that they represented only the stench of Fascism: and so I adopted an attitude of blind disgust.

I well knew this was a criminal trial. The SS men were being tried for criminal offences in Auschwitz. But my comrades and I also understood where the trial was being conducted, who was being tried, who the judges were, and who stood behind the court and the accused. But we also saw that hundreds of people were following events in the overcrowded hall. Students, working class youths – Germans of all ages – were hearing about the monstrous crimes committed in Auschwitz with bated breath. For them, as well as for us, this was no ordinary trial . . .

Cross examination begins. I sit calmly, trying to keep my cool for the benefit of those around me: but my nerves are strained. I'm trying to understand the essence of the questions, answers and arguments from facial expressions and vocal intonation. The face of the Interpreter, Vera, is most animated. She's nervous and taking it hard. Questions and answers find eloquent reflection on her face: expressing joy, indignation, anger, contempt, by turns.

My heart is flooded with a feeling of sincere gratitude to this small, active woman, who has become so dear to me over the last few days. A Russian Pole, she graduated from university in Warsaw and has never seen Russia. During the occupation of Poland, after the death of her parents, she was taken away to Germany, living for many years in Frankfurt-am-Main. Vera loves the Motherland of her ancestors and feels keenly the tragic fate of those Russians killed in the concentration camp. Meanwhile, she literally worships us survivors, who only arrived from Russia several days ago. And we were touched by her support – sincere and open-hearted.

Vera had been impatiently awaiting our testimony. After all, we were the first Soviet witnesses of these monstrous misdeeds. Vera had been present at the trial from the very beginning (in her role as Staff Interpreter of the Criminal Jury of the State of Hessen), hearing testimonies of ex-prisoners from various countries. For this reason she was eager to hear us, her countrymen by ancestry. She was firmly confident that we would speak up more strongly than previous witnesses; that our testimonies would be more convincing; and that we would make additional exposures. We were also united by our convictions with regard to Fascism. Vera hated Fascism not only as a progressive person who had understood its essence, but also as a woman and a mother . . .

A question from the Interpreter interrupted my thoughts: 'Mister witness, did you say in your testimony that the defendant Stefan Baretzki was a Blockführer in the concentration camp in October–November 1941?'

'Yes, I confirm it.'

The Chairman of the Court leafed through pages of a book, handed to him at his request from the huge bookcase filled with documents relating to the investigation: 'The court possesses documents testifying that Baretzki appeared in the camp for the first time in July 1942.'

'They are false. In October 1941 Baretzki was already present in the camp.'

I hear an ingratiating voice from the left: 'Could the witness confirm that the defendant Stark was an officer?'

'Yes, I confirm it.'

A question from the right: 'And could you distinguish an SS soldier from an officer?'

'Yes.'

I'm answering firmly and confidently, but the question from the right puts me on my guard. I immediately recall a conversation in Berlin, at the office of a well known lawyer, Professor Kaul. He told me then: 'Take into account that a defendant's council is the greatest danger to the truth of testimony. It's capable of any dirty trick. Defence councils often ask questions, the real sense of which is not always clear to people inexperienced in jurisprudence. In cases like that my colleagues and I – the public prosecutors – will do their best to come to your aid.'

Again there is a clarifying question: 'Please describe the external signs of difference between a soldier and an officer.' I answer as confidently as before, but try to understand what is hidden in these elementary questions.

'What was the colour of the shoulder badges worn by officers?' comes from the left.

I have no time to answer before a question comes from the right: 'What kind of shoulder badges did Stark have?'

I catch from Vera's eyes that she is on guard. There is something wrong here. 'Calm down, calm down,' I mentally tell myself. Straining my memory, I answer with uncertainty: 'It's hard to recall such a detail, for during that horrible time it wasn't my concern. But it seems to me that Stark had badges that were not fully silver but with silver edging.'

A buzz sweeps over the hall. The Chairman raises his knitted eyebrows. Vera's face sparkles with joy. My memory hadn't let me down. It appeared that Stark – a Gestapo commissioner for Soviet POW affairs – was an NCO.

'Do you know the defendant Boger?'

'No.'

'And Kaduk?'

'No.'

'Scherpe?'

'I do. The last time I saw him and Klehr was in May or June 1942 in the hospital of Block 21. In front of almost all the patients Scherpe and Klehr murdered prisoners 'fitness-checked' by an SS doctor with phenol injections.'

'Can you draw a plan of the hospital and operating room, and show the spot from which you saw the phenol injections made?'

'Yes.'

I'm given a sheet of paper and quickly draw the location of Blocks 10, 11 and 21. I drew a plan of the hospital, showing the surgical room, the doctors' corner, and the spot where I found myself a witness to the terrible murder. The Interpreter handed the plan to the Chairman. The defenders of the accused and the public prosecutors stood up to see the plan. They brought another plan, compared them, and fell into discussion.

'The plan of the inner layout of the hospital made by you is somewhat different from the one possessed by the court,' said Hofmeyer, the Chairman of the Court.

'Possibly I drew a plan as it was in the summer of 1942. The court obviously has a plan from 1945.'

'The court will add the plan to the trial documents.'

After several insignificant questions from the defence, which I answered as confidently as before, they stopped interrogating me, understanding that the answers would only harm the interests of their clients. I sighed, freer, when suddenly: 'Mister Chairman suggests you identify the accused.'

Noise, tapping, coughing came from the left as the accused stood up. A thought flashed: refuse under any pretext! No, as an ex-prisoner of Auschwitz and a witness from the USSR I can't refuse! After all, I'd been giving testimony not only on behalf of myself, not only on behalf of those who'd miraculously survived, but also on behalf of the many thousands of prisoners who'd died terrible, excruciating deaths. The memory of the murdered and the hope of the living obliged me to disregard my personal wishes: so I resolutely turned to the accused for the first time.

But as soon as I glanced at them I became flustered – and so badly that I felt hot all over. Surrounded by guards, the accused stood before me in three rows. Dressed in brand-new suits, clean-shaven with well-groomed faces, sleek hair perfectly parted, they stood like gentlemen who'd accidentally strayed into the hall from a banquet or ceremonial reception. They scrutinized me defiantly, smiling with contempt and malice, but with no trace of their former bombast and pomposity. If one didn't know better, one might have taken them for decent folk: but each one might have bathed in the blood of his victims. For with each step they had sowed death; with every movement they'd spilled blood; with every wave of the hand or glance of the eye they'd unleashed murder. But now they were no longer wearing green and black uniforms but fashionable suits, with handkerchiefs coquettishly sticking out of breast pockets. And yet, in their squinting eyes and twitching mouths one could detect the bestial hatred of Fascist butchers and sadists. How could they look me in the face and smile? For I stood before them as a witness to their crimes. I embodied the weeping children, the moaning mothers, the helpless fathers. Yes, I embodied the blood and ashes of millions. Only a wild beast can calmly look into the eyes of its prey . . .

Several times I ran my eyes over the faces of former SS men. But a hot, heart-wrenching sensation of confusion was creeping over me, stronger and stronger. My back grew wet, my face was burning, my hands broke out in a cold sweat. The fact remained that I could recognize no one out of the accused men quietly scrutinizing me. No one! Not even those against whom I was just giving testimony. More than twenty years had passed since that terrible time. The years and clothes had changed their appearance. I burrowed into their faces, trying to catch at least something that might give a hint, but all my efforts were in vain. The realization of my powerlessness intensified the confusion. I felt unable to hide my condition, and saw a flicker of triumph on the Fascists' faces.

I made a final attempt with an effort of will, bowing my head, screwing up my eyes and covering my face with my hands. 'You have to recall, you have to recall!' I was telling myself, in time with my heartbeats. Meanwhile the audience froze. Breaking the palpable silence came the booming sound of approaching steps: 'Are you unwell?' The questions of the Chairman and Interpreter rang out almost simultaneously. I turned to the court, raised my head, then took my hands off my face. A policeman was standing in front of me with a glass of water. The expression on his face bespoke both alarm and sincere commiseration. I cleared my throat: 'Yes, it's hard to revive the memory of faces more than twenty years later. I covered my face so as to imagine them young, in uniform . . .'

The Deputy Chairman whispered something to the Chairman, gesticulating with conviction. Hofmeyer listened gloomily, then nodded in agreement and barked several words at the accused. I had no time to catch their meaning when I saw four of the accused step down by order of a guard and take position behind me, facing the court. Vera translated the Chairman's command with shining eyes: 'In order to ease identification, the court has deemed it possible to change the customary order. The accused will be stepping forward into the hall by fours.'

I turned around and scrutinized each of them separately. In the centre of the hall they looked completely different than in the bright beams of floodlights. The expressions on their faces had changed too. Grimaces and contemptuous grins had disappeared, and despite the feigned indifference to all that was happening, their eyes betrayed both hatred and fear. The passing years had changed nothing: these were enemies standing before me.

My confidence returned. Among the first four criminals who stepped out I recognized no one I'd met before, despite the keenest inspection. But when scrutinizing the next four I caught some kind of nervousness in the third man. Some barely conscious signal struck me, attracting my attention. Although I was standing in front of the second man, I was unable to take my eyes off the third, who was clearly uncomfortable. Ageing, obese, with a large bald patch above his retreating forehead, he was shifting from one foot to the other. Suddenly he pulled a folded handkerchief out of his pocket and patted his bald patch with a practised movement. This gesture reminded me of something. Yes, yes, something nightmarish was connected with it. My heart shrank at some kind of premonition, the blood pounding in my temples. Noticing my emotions the third man produced his handkerchief again, shook it out, and returned to patting the bald patch, now shining with perspiration. A recollection flashed like lightning: a stuffy room, a hundred naked, emaciated prisoners moving towards a desk, where a careless nod of the head or a languid movement of the finger by the SS medico will decide the fate of each of them . . . Bright sun spreading light and warmth in the hospital operating theatre, a fat SS officer is bending over another victim, syringe in hand . . . Klehr? Klehr! 'It's Klehr!'

Agitated by the first encounter I supported my weight on a desk, unable to see or hear anything clearly. The next quartet stepped out behind me. 'The judge requests you to continue the identification.' Oppressed in body and soul, I automatically spun around. A man aged about forty-five met my gaze. Elegantly dressed, sunglasses in hand, he stood before me with an arrogant expression on his face. But the more I stared, the more my confidence grew: I knew this man. The association of many features – height, shape of head, expression of eyes, outline of nose and lips – revived in my memory a similar form, again connected with some painful episode of the distant past. A swarm of thoughts rushed through my mind. Without taking my eyes off him I dug into my memory, trying to link the features of the man before me with one of those who escorted us along the tragic Auschwitz path.

Discernment came in an instant, evoking a state of shock. My head swam, my skin prickled with sweat. Staggering, I leaned against the desk, willing myself to hold on, to come to my senses. A mischievous smile, flashing on the lips of the butcher, finally restored my strength. I felt ashamed of myself, of my weakness, revealed so unexpectedly. So this is you, the Commissioner for Soviet Citizens' Affairs? Was it you who murdered my comrade on the station square, over a photograph of his daughter – a little girl with a bow in her hair? Yesterday I heard that you'd concealed your past from your family; that your wife and two daughters only discovered your crimes here at the trial. Now, with one accord, they are disowning you as husband and father. People say you suffer this as a personal tragedy. But don't you think my comrade – the unknown soldier you killed – suffered separation from his family? And all thanks to your Fascist gods! Don't you think his heart bled for a daughter left behind? The little girl whose photo your SS-Mann trampled in the mud? No, neither you nor any like you belong on Earth. You should be shunned like lepers, branded – like your victims – so that everyone might see what you truly are: monsters who turned a town into Hell, tormenting, torturing, murdering millions in an empire devoted to death.

His eyelid trembled. I guessed he'd recognized me and his nerve was failing. Do you remember how once we were standing in front of each other? You could have killed me back then by a skilful blow on the bridge of my nose. But I survived. And despite all I endured, I remember you. I even recall the colour of your eyes. You feel nervous, don't you? The knots in your cheeks are twitching, just as they did before. I broke the protracted silence with a hoarse, faltering voice: 'Stark!'

A step to the side. Another man is in front of me. An oblong face. Restless eyes, nervous, twitching fingers. Ah! So you are together even here . . . 'This is Blockführer Baretzki.'

Three times the Chairman of the Court drew my attention away and in the meantime, behind my back, each man out of the four swapped places with another. But it was impossible to make a mistake and I successfully identified the guilty men each time.

My nervous condition, and the awkward business of place-swapping, had drawn my attention so fully that I heard a noise in the audience only after a peremptory shout from the Chairman. He stood up and demanded quiet in the hall with exasperation in his voice. The spectators were obviously excited by something. The policemen on duty appeared in front of the first row. But their arrival didn't restore calm. 'What's happening?' It was already 7pm – the seventh hour of my testimony – and well past the usual hours for court business. Perhaps people were tired and requesting a break? My thoughts were interrupted by the same embittered metallic-toned voice of Hofmeyer. The Interpreter answered my unspoken question: 'Herr Chairman of the Court is greatly outraged by the behaviour of the audience and has announced a break till tomorrow.'

But my assumptions proved incorrect. Most spectators were in no hurry to leave and crowded the narrow aisle through which I was trying to leave the hall. Vera walked ahead of me. Hundreds of eyes scrutinized me again, but not with simple curiosity as before: now they were possessed by the fire of emotion. With joy in my soul, I saw the goodwill, sympathy and approving smiles of the majority. The warm, friendly handshakes were affecting; while the right hands clenched into fists and raised to the shoulder were even more poignant. That night I slept for the first time in many days.

Epilogue

This morning the West German Court passed sentence on twenty SS criminals who acted in the biggest Nazi death camp Auschwitz during the War. The court sentenced the accused: Boger, Hoffman, Kaduk, Baretzki and Bednarek to life imprisonment. Eleven of the accused were sentenced to various terms from eight years and three months up to fourteen years. Three of the accused were acquitted. Further, the court decided to take into account time spent in pre-trial custody. This sentence was announced after a trial lasting exactly twenty months. About 360 eyewitnesses, mostly consisting of ex-prisoners of Auschwitz who evaded extermination only by a miracle, provided their testimony. The testimonies implicating the accused in commission of mass murder were given during the process by citizens of Poland, Czechoslovakia, the German Democratic Republic, the Federal Republic of Germany, Israel, the United States, France, Belgium and other countries. Some of the accused sent hundreds of prisoners to the gas chambers – men, women, old people, and children. The accused also took part in the shooting of prisoners, murdered them by injections into the heart etc. . . .

From 'Light Sentence for Nazi Murderers' – a TASS report dated Frankfurt-am-Main, 19 August 1965.

The national flags of dozens of countries surround a monument buried in live flowers. The air is full of funereal tunes and the buzz of a swarm of people. Representatives of many countries stand on the rostrum, next to a monument dedicated to the victims of Auschwitz. Among them there are tourists from the Soviet Union – former inmates – and delegates from the Soviet Committee of War Veterans, led by 'Hero of the Soviet Union' Lieutenant General Vasili Yakovlevich Petrenko, former commander of the division that liberated the camp on 27 January 1945. After a solemn, mournful ceremony of remembrance, the Soviet veterans visit the central camp. It's hard to breathe. It seems the air is full of burning smoke and soot from the crematorium . . .

I stood before the gates oppressed by sweeping recollections. The deserted watch towers do not threaten with machine-guns, no fierce shouts are heard, no emaciated shadows in striped clothing wander about the camp. The rest has been preserved untouched, as it used to be: the gates with the mocking inscription 'Arbeit Macht Frei' ('Freedom Through Labour'), the dense web of barbed-wire fences, two-storey buildings of red brick, the gas chambers, the gallows. Some documents, photographs, clothes, possessions, piles of female hair, children's prams, artificial limbs also survived: material evidence of crimes committed here, crimes previously unknown to humankind. Auschwitz is now a State Museum of the Polish People's Republic . . .

After visiting Block 11, I step into the inner yard, following the route of those condemned to death. On the right is a black rectangle of wall. It hypnotizes like the muzzle of a gun. My eyes don't blink – they are riveted to the black wall – the wall of monstrous torture, the wall of firing squads [the original 'Death Wall' was demolished before the end of the war but reconstructed by the Auschwitz Museum – trans.]. The rectangle looms closer and closer, squeezing out the sky, screening everything in front of me. And suddenly the wall comes alive. Figures began emerging: vaguely at first, then clearer, more distinctly. There are hundreds, thousands of them. The back rows are hidden in the hazy distance. There is one man in front. He looks at me intently. A spasmodic shiver runs down my back. My face and hands break out in a cold sweat. Of course it's Wilhelm Türschmidt. I couldn't fail to recognize him . . .

Don't look at me so sternly. I haven't forgotten. I've been remembering – I do remember – and will remember you till my dying day, till my heart stops beating. You're a doctor after all, and you'll understand the sincerity of my words better than anyone. Did you smile? You're happy that I haven't forgotten you? I remember everything as if it were yesterday. You called me a 'Russian Bolshevik' and I was proud of that. You snatched me from the cold clutches of death. But you didn't just save a guy called Andrzej [Polish for Andrei, the author's first name – trans.], you saved one of those Russian Bolsheviks whose extermination you were witnessing. And by saving me you expressed your sympathy with those Russian Bolsheviks who were defending freedom far in the East. Am I lying? No, it's true, it's true! I saw it very well back then and see it now in your squinted blue eyes, sparkling with love and respect. And you've hardly changed at all. The same deep wrinkles on your forehead, the same stern expression in your eyes, and the same dignified grey head.

I'm happy to advise you that you guessed correctly: I found my family. I have good daughters and already a grown-up grand-daughter. And they all know your name, for I've told them so much about the Chief Surgeon of Block 21: a man of great heart, the Polish political prisoner, Wilhelm Türschmidt.

If you only knew how hard it is for me sometimes. Especially when I'm remembering the children's screams from Block 10. We'd plug our ears with paper dressings. Once I saw you doing the same in the operating room. But was it really possible to muffle the moans of a dying child? His fading cry for help?

Do you remember those horrible days and nights? Your presence on quiet warm summer nights was necessary for us, the dozens of patients. It sowed fortitude in us, it helped us face the unthinkable, from which it was easy to go mad. You don't know, but we saw you during the last minutes of your heroic life.

Can you guess how? Of course, we stood behind the bunks in front of the windows. We were not seen but witnessed everything. No matter how hard it was to look, we – your colleagues and friends – couldn't turn our eyes from that tragic episode. We wept as only men could weep. We wept from awareness of our own feebleness, from hatred towards the butchers. But inwardly we were proud of your fortitude. You'd been a real patriot of your long-suffering Motherland up to the last minute. And you remained in our memories as such a man, and that's how I'm seeing you now . . .

I've just walked around the cells of Block 11. Grey walls, grey floor. The steps boom in the big, empty rooms. Images of the sadistic brutality played out here used to weigh heavily on our hearts and oppress our minds. It's impossible to imagine what you had to live through. You spent the last hours before your death in such a prison cell, didn't you? Of course you were tortured. You were not given a minute's rest. Oh! These butchers were highly proficient in their art, but were unable to understand the souls of those they tormented. They could kill bodies in a bout of fury, but were unable to break the spirits of their victims. These are your words, my dear father, brother and comrade. What, you're leaving? Where are you, for God's sake? I want to talk to you a bit more!

Don't resent me. I was lucky – I broke out of this hell. I survived. I'm infinitely happy that I lived to see the joyful day of Victory. But I haven't forgotten my experiences. And the passing of the years hasn't dulled the sharpness of the pain. The wounds of my body have healed over but the wounds in my heart remain deep. They will pain me for the rest of my life.

It's hard to say what sustained me through those inhuman ordeals: stamina, health, luck? What saved my soul in that hell, helped me carry my dreams, endeavours and love for the Motherland through the horrors of Auschwitz! Auschwitz! The whole world knows that name: the place where Fascists exterminated 4 million people from all over Europe in four years [although initially estimated at 4 million, the Auschwitz Museum later adjusted this figure to 1.5 million victims – trans.].

Leaving the Auschwitz Museum I, my fellow veterans, and all those who visit to gaze and wonder, carry away the same memento: a strong conviction that Fascism must not be permitted to rise again. And that the horrors of Auschwitz must never be repeated.

Glossary

Appell:	German camp term meaning 'roll-call'.
Appellplatz:	German camp term meaning 'roll-call area'.
Belogvardeyets:	Anti-Bolshevik White Guardsmen of the Russian Civil War (1918–22).
Blockälteste:	German camp term meaning 'block elder'. These men – who were themselves prisoners – supervized fellow inmates in their respective barrack blocks, being answerable to their 'Blockführer' (see below).
Blockführer:	German camp term meaning 'block commander'. These men occupied the lowest grade in the SS camp hierarchy, being responsible for controlling 'block elders' (see 'Blockälteste' above).
Gauleiter:	German term meaning 'regional leader'. A 'Gau' was a region of the Nazi Reich, a 'Gauleiter' its leading Nazi Party official.
Gestapo:	German contraction for 'Geheime Staatspolizei' or 'Secret State Police'.
Iron Cross:	Military decoration of Prussia and later Germany. The Iron Cross was awarded only in wartime for acts of bravery.
Kapo:	General camp term for a prisoner acting as an overseer. Kapos headed each work crew or labour battalion, larger formations having an 'Oberkapo' or 'senior overseer'.
Kolkhoz:	Russian term for a Soviet collective farm.

Kommando:	German camp term meaning 'work crew'. Some 300 work crews existed at Auschwitz, containing anything from 50 to 1,200 prisoners.
Kommandoführer:	German camp term meaning 'work crew commander'. These men were usually drawn from the ranks of the SS-Blockführers (see 'Blockführer' above).
Kommissar:	Soviet Communist Party official, responsible for political education and organization.
Kulak:	Russian term for wealthy, land-owning peasants, ruthlessly persecuted by the Stalinist regime.
Lagerführer:	German camp term meaning 'prison commander'. These SS officials were responsible for running the prisoners' compounds.
Moskal:	Pejorative Ukrainian nickname for a Russian.
'Muselmänner':	SS jargon for any feeble and emaciated prisoner, derived from the German word for 'Mussulman' or 'Muslim'. The origin of the term is thought to lie in the comparison between wobbly, skeletal prisoners hardly capable of standing, and the repeated nodding and prostration of Muslims at prayer.
Nemetchina:	Russian word meaning 'Germany'.
Oberführer:	Paramilitary rank of the German Nazi Party, roughly translated as 'senior leader'.
Oberkorporal:	German military rank, roughly translated as 'senior corporal'.
Osobi otdel:	Security unit of a Soviet military or Partisan unit.
Pan:	Polish term meaning 'mister' or 'sir'.
Pentka:	Camp term for the partitioned compartment of a large hall, derived from the Polish word 'piąty', meaning 'one-fifth'.
Politruk:	Russian term meaning 'political commissar'.
Polizei:	Term for a German-organized police force of collaborationists, active in German-occupied territory.
Schreiber:	German term meaning 'clerk'. The 'Blockschreiber' was responsible for checking the precise number of prisoners in a block. The 'Schreiberführer' acted as 'head clerk'.
Sedemka:	Camp term for 'Block 7', derived from the Polish word 'siódemka', meaning 'seventh'.

Sonderführer:	German camp term denoting the leader of a 'Sonderkommando' (see below).
Sonderkommando:	German camp term meaning 'special unit' or 'special squad'. Such work crews were responsible for cleaning gas chambers of human excrement and blood, removing hair, gold teeth and jewellery from corpses, burning corpses and digging mass graves.
Sovkhoz:	Russian term for a state-owned farm.
SS:	German acronym of 'Schutzstaffel' or 'protection squad'. Formed in 1925 as Hitler's bodyguard, this paramilitary force grew into a huge organization which, among other duties, provided death camp guards.
SS-Mann:	Lowest rank of the paramilitary SS, roughly equivalent to an Army private.
Starshina:	Russian term meaning 'sergeant major'.
Taiga:	Russian term for vast expanses of primeval forest.
TASS:	Official news agency of the Soviet Union.
Tovarishch:	Russian slang term for 'comrade'.
Voencomat:	Soviet commissariat office in charge of military affairs for a given district.
Vorarbeiter:	German camp term meaning 'foreman'.
Zyklon-B:	Although other death camps used carbon monoxide for mass murders, Auschwitz employed 'Zyklon-B' – a cyanide gas made from prussic acid, originally used as a common insecticide.

Index